Treasury of
Käthe Kruse Dolls

Album 3

Lydia Richter

Popular *Träumerchen* from 1925.

Treasury of
Käthe Kruse Dolls

Album 3

HPBooks

Doll apartment with bears, dogs, rabbits and things to delight a child's heart. Child loves her Käthe Kruse doll, Beate.

Publisher: Rick Bailey
Editorial Director: Randy Summerlin
Editor: Susan Luzader Prust
Art Director: Don Burton
Book Assembly: Barry Myers
Typography: Cindy Coatsworth, Michelle Claridge
Translation: David Woloshin, Ph.D.
Technical Consultant: Mildred Seeley

HPBooks®
P.O. Box 5367
Tucson, Arizona 85703
(602) 888-2150
ISBN: 0-89586-331-6
Library of Congress Catalog Card Number: 84-80437
©1984 Fisher Publishing Inc.
Printed in U.S.A.

Originally published in Germany as Käthe Kruse Puppen: Puppen Album 3.
©1982, 1983 by Verlag Laterna magica GmbH and Co.

ACKNOWLEDGMENTS
The author is grateful to Sofie Rehbinder-Kruse for information and the loan of important documents and historical photographs. Mrs. Rehbinder-Kruse wrote the text on pages 52 and 53. The Stalling family provided several old company brochures and photos from their collection. Additional thanks go to Liz Körle, Mrs. Schweiger, Mrs. von Eicken, Mrs. Neuback and Mrs. Hauert for the loan of their dolls. Special thanks go to Mrs. Gottschalk and others who made historical information available. Mrs. Stangl and Mrs. Driskell made reproductions of some doll clothing.
Text source: Käthe Kruse, The Great Doll Game, I and My Dolls and Kuddelmuddel; and firm brochures.
Photographs: All photographs are by Lydia Richter, except those on pages 76, 97, 107 center right, 109 center left and 114 by Fred Stalling. Pages 118, 119 by Sofie Rehbinder-Kruse. Pages 99 center and top and page 115 are factory photographs. Historical black-and-white photos were made by Käthe, Sofie, Jochen and Max Kruse. Others are factory photos. Torsten Rehbinder made the portrait of his 81-year-old grandmother, Käthe Kruse, on page 35.

Käthe Kruse surrounded by her dolls.

TABLE OF CONTENTS

Doll I in historical costume from 1920s.

Das Herz erfüllt voll Sonnenschein,
Lustwandeln sie beglückt zu zwei'n.

Hand-colored Käthe Kruse post card from Jan. 21, 1918. Shows two examples of *Doll I* as loving couple.

Hampelchen, Doll XII.

My Quest For Answers

For as long as I have been an enthusiastic collector of Käthe Kruse dolls, I have always been curious about the many unanswered questions concerning these charming doll children. I learned very quickly there are many collectors who couldn't supply answers either.

So I began the intense and exciting task of answering these questions. In doing so, I had the great good fortune of meeting the second daughter of Käthe Kruse, Sofie Rehbinder-Kruse. We began collaborating and she gave me authentic historical materials. She gave me the original pattern of the head and body of *Doll I* and the original 1910 contract with Kämmer & Reinhardt about the manufacture of Käthe Kruse dolls. She also provided many unpublished photos and other documents appearing in this book. The plan for this book began to take shape.

Actually, everything began very innocently. Several years ago at a doll auction, I fell in love with a Käthe Kruse doll. It stood simply and modestly with its little red cheeks in unadorned pajamas at the edge of a table. In spite of that, it was able to claim attention among all the refined, pale porcelain beauties wrapped in silk and lace. As I repeatedly went up and down the rows, its sweet round face kept coming back to me.

I couldn't resist this doll, so I bought the 1927 *Schlenkerchen*. Later, when I began to do a bit of research, I learned that I had actually bought a *Hampelchen* that was approximately 10 years younger. But that didn't make me love it any less.

However, I didn't first discover my love for these beautiful cloth dolls at the auction. I had been attracted to them years earlier. Indeed, I already owned two carefully protected Kruse children that I had received as a gift from my mother in the early 1950s. Unfortunately, I found out that one of the dolls had a plastic head.

When I encountered the old Kruse dolls with their inimitable radiant nature, my interest was rekindled. Suddenly I wanted to know everything about Käthe Kruse and her beautiful cloth dolls. I enthusiastically researched all books as well as newspaper and magazine articles on the topic. I asked many collectors and dealers about the dolls. I compared and studied all the dolls I could find.

Because I didn't know much about the dolls, each piece of information was special. Soon, however, the gaps in my new knowledge became evident. No one could give satisfactory answers to my more specialized questions.

Even worse, no other doll was the object of so much contradictory information. Käthe Kruse dolls also had many unbelievable stories about them. There was, for example, the matter of the running numbers on the sole of the foot. Many collectors swear these numbers are continuous and one can tell the age of the doll from them. Some claim there were about 20 to 50 different head types. Others say a considerably larger number.

And there was nothing at all precise to be learned about the age of individual dolls. I was told all dolls with painted hair were the first or earliest. Heads have had painted hair continuously and are still made today. Even the later dolls with wigs were, as a rule, considered to be 10 to 20 years older.

Good fortune came to my aid when I was able to obtain the book *The Great Doll Game* that Käthe Kruse wrote in 1956. I immediately read the book several times. I was fascinated by the life of this marvelous woman with her seven children and her husband, the sculptor, Professor Max Kruse. From this I was able to collect the first exact information concerning the dolls.

After evaluating newspaper clippings about Käthe Kruse and her dolls, I decided to treat them with great caution because they are not always accurate.

I went to Donauwörth, the present location of the Kruse workshops. I had hoped to do research about the early dolls where they originated. This visit, however, was very disappointing. I did not get to look at any old dolls, and except for a few bits of information, I learned only that all important documents concerning the Käthe Kruse dolls had been left behind in Bad Kösen.

I was able to make another step forward when I received photocopies of brochures from the years 1927-1928 and 1929-1930. They were only legible with a magnifying glass. Here I learned that only documents published by the Kruse workshops could furnish precise details concerning the famous dolls.

Next I looked for source material in antique book stores and advertised in trade publications. This was without success until enthusiastic collectors of Käthe Kruse dolls began to give me some original catalogs.

In spite of that, this book would not have been complete if I hadn't been successful in gaining the cooperation of Sofie Rehbinder-Kruse. She was the decisive factor in the writing of this book.

The 78-year-old, second-oldest daughter of Käthe Kruse was my closest collaborator. She entered the family business as an apprentice at 14, learned everything from the ground up and was later the director and agent for the business for many years.

She was highly gifted artistically and created many of the heads for the beautiful Kruse Show-Window Dolls. To my great joy, she was immediately prepared to collaborate and supported me without reservation during my work. This is true especially with regard to the acquisition of historical documents and information. Mrs. Rehbinder-Kruse has definitely helped me in the realization of this book, and she has my deepest gratitude.

My thanks also to those who permitted me to photograph their dolls. I'm also very grateful to those who helped with old brochures and other valuable documentation.

Lydia Richter

Du Mein, in its original Bogyman costume. It was created about 1925 and became very successful. This doll had painted hair but was available beginning in 1930 with a human-hair wig.

Above: *Doll I* with painted hair, in original clothing as Red Riding Hood.

Left: Two *Doll VIII*s enjoying a sleigh ride.

Above: Doll wedding. Opposite page: Two dolls in native costumes in Bavarian mountains.

Above: Vacation in the country. Opposite page: *Hampelchen's* walk in the rain. Reproduced from an old brochure.

Above: Forest festival. Opposite page: Baby *Du Mein* as it looks at the world.

Margaretchen and Jockerle

Doll I, original Käthe Kruse doll as it was manufactured until 1952. It is shown in four popular models with clothing reconstructed from original.

Red Riding Hood　　　　　　　　　　**German Michel**

The Great Doll Adventure

The career of Katharina Simon, who was born in Breslau in 1833, had been mapped out. Immediately after finishing school at 16, she began acting lessons from Otto Gerlach of the Breslau City Theatre. At 17, she was already employed by the Lessing Theatre in Berlin for 250 marks a month. That was a lot of money at the time.

Her guest performances in Warsaw and Moscow seemed to be opening a promising career for the young actress. She played the role of Käthchen in *The Slave* by Ludwig Fulda, of Gisa Holm in *Flachsmann as Educator* by Otto Ernst, and of Hannele in Gerhart Hauptmann's *Hannele's Ascension*. She assumed the stage name of Hedda Somin.

She became acquainted with the Berlin sculptor Max Kruse when she was 19. He had been honored with a gold medal at the Berlin art exhibit for his famous work, *The Victory Message of Marathon*. He created busts of Max Liebermann, Gerhart Hauptmann, Henrik Ibsen and many others. He especially loved the feel of wood for his sculptures. Kruse had aired his profound and practical philosophy in such books as *A Path to New Forms* and *The Education of the Child Through Three-Dimensional Vision*. The man Katharina Simon met in Berlin was more than a respected sculptor and author. More about him later.

Max Kruse and Katharina Simon developed a profound relationship after meeting at a table of artists in the Cafe of the West. They married

Käthe Kruse as a 7-year-old in Breslau.

Right: Young actress Katharina (Käthe) Simon, who used the stage name Hedda Somin. She was a guest performer at 18 in Warsaw and Moscow. A year later, she married sculptor Max Kruse.

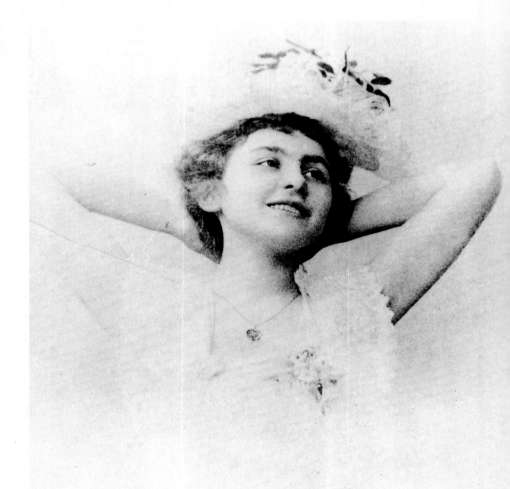

and their relationship produced seven children. An eighth died shortly after birth.

The attraction and marriage allowed enough freedom for both to develop their personalities and creativity. This great love lasted for a lifetime and saw Käthe Kruse become a doll legend. It also had positive influences on the great artist-professor Max Kruse.

Käthe Kruse had to give up her acting to prepare for her new role as a mother. Her first child, Maria, born in December 1902, was nicknamed *Mimerle*. One year later, she gave birth to Sofie, her second daughter, who was nicknamed *Fifi*.

Sofie joined her mother's business at age 14. She stayed and eventually served as business director and agent for the Kruse workshops for 30 years. Sofie represented the second generation of Kruses with her great artistic gift and well-developed sense of the practical. She, as well as her siblings, inherited many talents from their parents.

For example, without any training, Sofie Kruse created an excellent bust of her brother, Friedebald. She created almost all the later Show-Window Doll heads and constructed the ball-joint skeleton for life-size Show-Window Dolls. We will discuss Sofie and her brothers and sisters later.

Käthe Kruse as an actress.

Shortly before the birth of Sofie, Max Kruse decided his children should not grow up in the big city of Berlin. The intense search for a suitable home led to the city of Ascona, Switzerland. Kruse kept his artist's studio in Berlin. Visits back and forth always became a pleasant family experience with trips to Zurich, Geneva and Lugano. This continued for years.

Although the two girls, Maria and Sofie, demanded much of their mother's time, Käthe Kruse developed astonishing talents. She began to study philosophy, paint, photograph, draw and learn Italian. With what time she had left over, she wrote about everything she learned, experienced, thought and felt.

Whenever Käthe Kruse took care of little Sofie, Maria looked on and was deeply impressed.

It was natural the 3-year-old should say to her mother, "I would also like to have a child like you and Mother Mary."

Käthe Kruse discovered her talent as a hobby painter in Ascona, Switzerland.

Käthe decided her daughter needed a doll. She had never been wild about dolls as a child, but now she became attracted to them. She asked her husband to buy a doll. He discovered the cold and fragile bisque porcelain dolls were not suitable as playthings. His daughter wouldn't be able to treat a doll like a genuine baby and caress it and hold it. He told his wife, "I'll not buy you dolls. I find them awful. Make some yourself." This comment was to be published many times in newspapers.

The dolls Käthe developed between 1906 and 1910 were exclusively for her daughters. A knotted towel was the first body. It was filled with sand and a potato was tied to the longer side of the towel as the head. Eyes, mouth and nostrils were marked by burned matches.

Above: Maria and Sofie, the first Käthe Kruse doll mothers. Potato-head faces were replaced with a stitched mask. Doll bodies were filled with cotton batting or sawdust.

Right: First doll in 1906. Käthe Kruse was inspired by her husband to make dolls for her daughters, Maria and Sofie. The head was a potato. The body was tied into a knotted handkerchief filled with sand. Eyes, mouth and nostrils were drawn with a burned match. The doll carriage was made at home. The photograph was made with a plate camera and developed at home. Käthe Kruse was an enthusiastic amateur photographer.

Maria loved these first dolls as much as Sofie later loved the doll Oscar. This doll had a definite shape and weighed less. The body was cut from nettle cloth filled with shavings. It was designed after a plaster model of the Christ Child by Verocchio.

Käthe Kruse had to make improved versions as the older ones wore out. Soon there was a new doll for every birthday or other occasion. The children loved this. But friends, acquaintances and neighbors kept saying, "Why doesn't Kruse buy his children decent dolls?"

Käthe improved most aspects of the dolls, but still had trouble with the noses. She didn't solve the problem in her amateur days of doll making. But she did enjoy this activity more and more.

Her third daughter, Johanna, was born in 1909. She was nicknamed *Hanne* or *Hannerle.* One year later her husband sculpted a very well-known bust of Maria in Ascona.

While staying in Munich in 1910, Käthe Kruse found a head by a Flemish sculptor. She covered it with cloth, then filled the covering with wax. She painted the resulting head. These dolls still had nothing to do with the Käthe Kruse dolls we know. This Flemish head was probably the model for *Doll I.*

Käthe Kruse's doll philosophy developed as the dolls did. She felt dolls should be primitive and natural. She unintentionally developed a new doll type as she made her children's toys. In 1910, she was surprised to be invited to participate in an exhibition called *Homemade Toys* in the Tietz department store in Berlin.

She felt her children's dolls were not suited for display because they looked worn out. She also had not solved the nose problem. She made new dolls and tried to decide if she should ask her husband for help.

Above: Maria and Sofie with their dolls.
The painting was done by their mother.

Left: Classically arranged portrait of
Käthe Kruse, Maria and Sofie in 1909.

As a sculptor, he should easily be able to fix the noses with no trouble, she thought. She convinced him to help form a head with the nose, ears and mouth. Then the dolls were ready for display.

This exhibition began a new part of Käthe Kruse's life. She scored a private success and began the public recognition of her dolls. Her husband had started the doll project and made an artistic contribution. She was on her way to becoming a famous doll maker.

Enthusiastic mothers came to the Kruse apartment after the exhibition to order dolls. The Kruses were not prepared for this or for the interest of doll manufacturers. They knew they needed to take advantage of the public's interest even if they didn't have a workshop.

The Kruses signed a contract on Dec. 29, 1910, with doll manufacturer Kämmer & Reinhardt. The contract is shown on page 22. The firm was permitted to manufacture and distribute Käthe Kruse dolls.

Käthe Kruse was paid 5,000 marks, a large sum for the time. The amount was doubled when Max Kruse got the patent for the invention and manufacture of dolls' heads. The contract also gave a commission of 1 mark for each doll sold.

The contract was extraordinarily good, but Käthe Kruse didn't believe the dolls Kämmer & Reinhardt made were up to her standards. She was sure her ideas were good, and she was concerned about quality. She wrote, "They sent them to me for approval. They weren't pretty. They were blue-pink as though they stood outside and were freezing mercilessly. The bodies were wide and clumsy. They looked like pumped-up flounders. The legs were stuffed with kapok and blown up like air pillows. Everything was worked out more precisely and carefully than I ever could have done it. But, I found them horrible. Horrible,

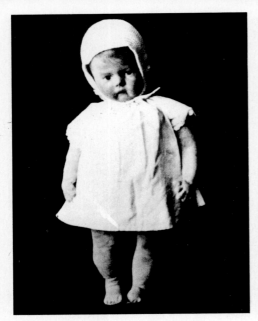

First Käthe Kruse play doll in 1911.

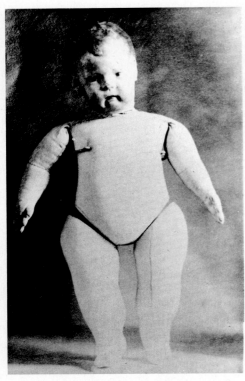

Doll I by Kämmer & Reinhardt. It was manufactured for a few months in 1911. The clumsy body, called the *flounder look,* was typical. In rare cases, ball joints were used in the knees. See page 102.

blond, narrow heads with bright blue eyes sat on long, thin necks on blue, frozen, fat bodies."

Letters, discussions and advice couldn't solve the problem. An agreement permitted Kämmer & Reinhardt to produced Käthe Kruse dolls for a few months of 1911. Kämmer & Reinhardt got their money back and Käthe Kruse received her patterns and forms. A short-term manufacturing experiment with Fischer, Naumann & Co. in Ilmenau, Germany was not successful either.

Her luck changed when 150 dolls were ordered from America. They were to be delivered on Nov. 8, 1911.

Käthe Kruse had to do it herself. She turned the living room and every available space of her Berlin apartment into an improvised workshop. She employed five women, the painter Beyer and a few people who worked in their homes. They began cutting, sewing, stuffing and painting hair and faces. Everyone worked enthusiastically almost around the clock. Max Kruse helped by molding the heads.

They finished on time and the first 150 dolls were shipped to America. By Christmas 1911, the dolls had homes with families from Boston to Philadelphia, from New York to San Francisco. This was the beginning.

An order for 500 more dolls followed. Europeans began demanding the dolls. The Kruses had to find a workshop and equip it professionally. They started a search that ended in 1912 at Bad Kösen, Germany. The soon-to-be-famous Käthe Kruse dolls had begun their march around the world.

Doll I, created in 1911, established the fame of the Kruse dolls. The head of all Kruse dolls produced until 1922 was always that of *Doll I.* All have the same head no matter what name the doll bears or whether it is a boy or a girl. Not many doll collectors know this. The dolls appear different because they were hand-painted and wore different clothes.

World War I gave the young business in Bad Kösen lots of problems. The business began manufacturing small Soldier Dolls, called *Field Grays.* An example is shown on page 25. They were called *Potsdam Soldiers.* Making them provided an excuse to hold onto jobs during the war even though it was a questionable business move.

A wire skeleton, similar to the ones used by sculptors, was developed to provide better mobility. This little skeleton was very important later for *Schlenkerchen,* the Doll-Room Dolls, *Träumerchen* and the Kruse Show-Window Dolls. The Soldier Dolls were 4-1/2 inches (11cm) tall and only a few were made. They are extremely rare today. *Doll I* was also outfitted with uniforms. Photographs are on page 25.

Doll-Room Dolls were manufactured by the Kruse workshops from 1915 until about 1925. They were 4 inches (10cm) tall and had natural-looking faces. Only a few were made because they were so expensive. They had a wire skeleton similar to the Little Soldiers to provide flexibility and mobility.

Käthe Kruse first modeled the heads of the Doll-Room Dolls after portrait busts Max Kruse made of his parents, siblings and children.

Top: The Kruses were a stately family in 1914. Max and Käthe with Sofie and Maria, standing, and Michael, Jochen and Johanna.

Left and above: *Doll I* in post card scenes postmarked 1914 and 1917.

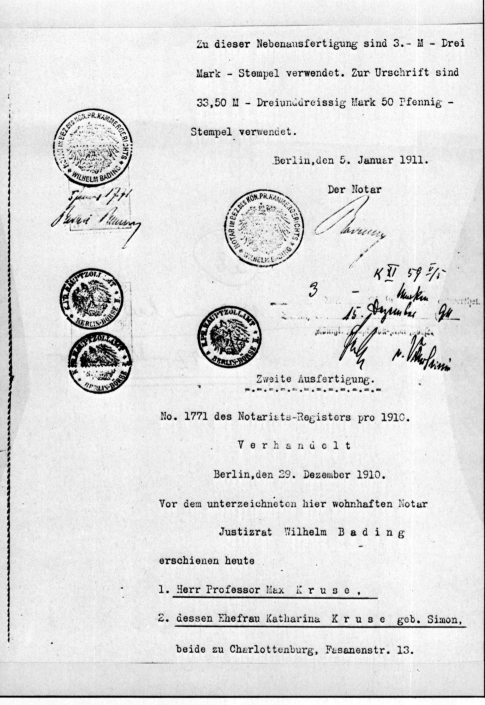

Excerpt from Dec. 29, 1910, contract between the Kruses and Kämmer & Reinhardt. Excellent contract conditions and careful preparation didn't prevent Käthe Kruse from canceling the deal. Kämmer & Reinhardt made Kruse dolls for a few months in 1911. She decided they weren't "pretty enough" for her.

Opposite page: *Doll I* received a gold medal at an international exhibition in Florence. It was the first year of production.

Eventually, peasant families, fairy-tale groups, coachmen, furniture movers and others were created. These were extremely expressive little dolls proportioned for the popular doll rooms of that time. They must have attracted lots of attention. These dolls were made entirely by hand and became too expensive to make.

This book is dedicated to the collector. To be complete, the soldiers and the Doll-Room Dolls must be mentioned. But they have nothing to do with the well-known Käthe Kruse play dolls, such as *Doll I* and its brothers and sisters.

A new doll type arrived with the creation of *Doll II, Schlenkerchen* in 1922. It smiled with an open-closed mouth, had a soft-wrapped body and loosely attached arms and legs. It was 13 inches (33cm) tall. This doll had the wire skeleton of the Little Soldiers.

Käthe=Kruse=Puppe

Gekleidet von Frau Anne Kurreck, Landsberg a. Lech

Nr. 18.

Nr. 30

Nr. 1.

Nr. 6

Nr. 8

Nr. 29

Nr. 22

Nr. 20

Nr. 32

Nr. 5

Nr. 3

Original=Aufnahmen vom Atelier „Veritas" München.

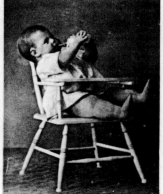

Nr. 1

Nr. 4

Jede Art Nachbildung gesetzlich verboten.

Große goldene Medaille
Internationale
Puppenausstellung Florenz 1911

23

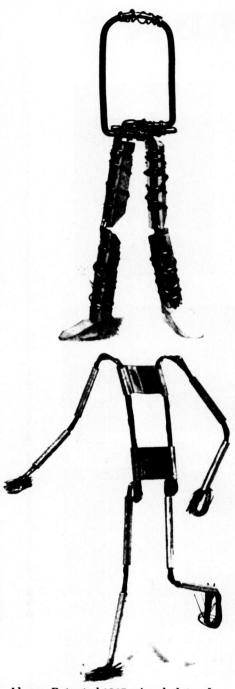

Above: Patented 1915 wire skeleton for the Little Soldier. Wire skeleton was used in 1922 for *Schlenkerchen* and in 1925 for *Träumerchen/Du Mein.* It was used in a modified form for the child-size Show-Window Dolls.

Above right: Magazine photo of soldier with handwritten notes by Käthe Kruse. In 1914, under dominance of Emperor Wilhelm II, people demanded Käthe Kruse make uniforms for her dolls. Many Germans greeted the war with cheers and flowers. The *Potsdam Soldier* was the result. Käthe Kruse developed a wire skeleton because children were tired of playing with stiff, tin soldiers. This doll soldier played an important role in developing other Kruse dolls with wire skeletons.

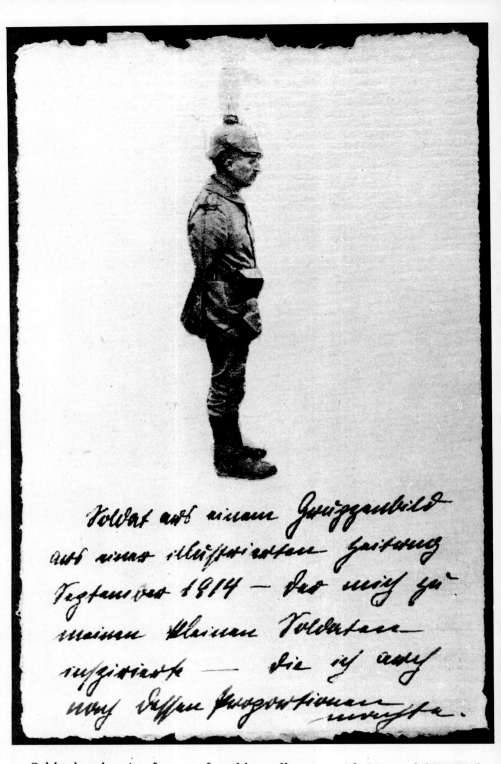

Schlenkerchen is often confused by collectors with *Hampelchen*. Both have flexible, attached arms and legs. *Hampelchen* was first produced in 1930. It does not smile and is not 13 inches (33cm) tall, as is the genuine *Schlenkerchen*.

The two bodies are quite different. *Schlenkerchen's* is softly wrapped over a skeleton with cotton batting and gauze and is always covered by tricot. *Hampelchen* was stuffed with deer or reindeer hair in a skin sewn of nettle cloth. It had stiff knees.

Kruse dolls were made with hair after 1928. Most have hand-knotted human-hair wigs, although dolls with painted hair are still manufactured by the Kruse workshops.

The motive for human-hair wigs was provided by a new branch of the

DIE POTSDAMER SOLDATEN VON KÄTHE KRUSE

11 cm hoch, weich, Einzelpreis 2 M. und 2.50 M., laffen fich in jede Stellung bringen.

Deutfche, Öfterreicher, Serben, Ruffen, Belgier, Franzofen, Engländer, Kolonialfoldaten

in einfchlägigen Gefchäften oder durch die

WERKSTÄTTE DER KÄTHE KRUSE-PUPPEN, BAD KÖSEN (SAALE)

Preisbuch mit zahlreichen Bildern und Zufammenftellungen gegen 35 Pf. (45 Heller) in Marken

Die großen Käthe Krufe-Puppen in Feldgrau!

(Preiskarte hiervon 10 Pfennig.) + Höhe 43 cm. Als Hemdmatzen 25 Mark. Das Katalog-Bilderbuch gegen Einfendung von 50 Pf. (60 Heller) in Marken.

Top left: Scenes show 4-1/2-inch (11cm) Field Grays called *Potsdam Soldiers.* Dolls could be set in various positions because of wire skeletons.

Left: Advertisement for *Potsdam Soldiers* published in December 1915.

Above: *Doll I* was clothed in uniform during World War I. Here it is presented on Käthe Kruse post cards.

Below *Doll I* photos: Ad for dolls from 1915. The price was 25 marks without a uniform.

doll industry. This was developed beginning in 1928 by the Kruse workshops in Bad Kösen. Käthe Kruse received a letter from a department store in Munich asking her to manufacture more dolls. The store owners wanted to decorate a show window with children for Mother's Day.

It was not an easy order because the dolls had to be flexible and able to stand. They also needed real hair like children. Human-hair wigs were made. Making the play dolls larger wasn't possible. The skeleton created in 1914-1915 for the Little Soldiers was enlarged for the child Show-Window Dolls. Larger child and adult Show-Window Dolls with ball joints and other important details were later developed. All this required much experimenting.

Käthe Kruse in 1925 with *Dolls I, II* and *V.*

Above and right: Käthe Kruse developed the 4-inch (10cm) Doll-Room Dolls in 1915. Their heads were realistically sculpted of plaster. They were flexible because of wire skeletons. The ballet scene in the doll-room picture shows this. Gentry coachman, porters, hotel figures and characters from *Hansel and Gretel* were presented in a 1916 magazine as the new flexible dolls by Käthe Kruse.

The child-size Kruse Show-Window Doll was produced beginning in 1928. The adult Show-Window Dolls began production in 1933. Many types and sizes were created. They range from the small child to the young lady and young gentleman. Kruse's son, Jochen, was most responsible for the appearance of these Show-Window Dolls. He had been trained in a Berlin silk shop as a window decorator. He was the most familiar of the Kruses with this industry and its needs. He loved the dolls he dressed. He gave their figures the flare of cultivated women and eventually provided them with a suitable husband.

As mentioned, almost all the heads were created by daughter Sofie. She made several of them. Her artistic gifts and her ability to sculpt were inherited from and encouraged by her parents.

She later invented a modeling material called *Fimoik*. It was an abbreviation for Fifi's mosaic. It is prized today by restoration specialists. This material is currently sold by the Eberhard Faber firm under the trademark *Fimo.*

Beginning in 1925, *Träumerchen, Du Mein* and *Friedebald/The German Child* were very successful. Käthe Kruse and Sofie traveled throughout the world recruiting sales representatives. This provided international distribution.

At its height, the enterprise employed 120 workers. It always remained a small artisanlike business. Käthe Kruse's greatest pride was the careful handwork of the dolls.

World War II had little effect on the Kruse workshop. The business

Doll II, Schlenkerchen, came out in 1922. It had a smiling face, open-closed mouth, painted hair, wire skeleton, loosely stitched arms and legs and tricot body covering. It was 13 inches (33cm) tall. *Mechanical Aid* could be the title of three sporty *Schlenkerchen* in the picture book *Play and Sport.*

Above: Käthe Kruse with her son, Friedebald, around 1922.

Right: Friedebald, born Aug. 15, 1918, received his name because peace was near. *Bald* means *soon* and *friede* means *peace.* **The family hoped the horror of World War I would soon end. He died at the age of 27 shortly before the end of World War II in a military accident.**

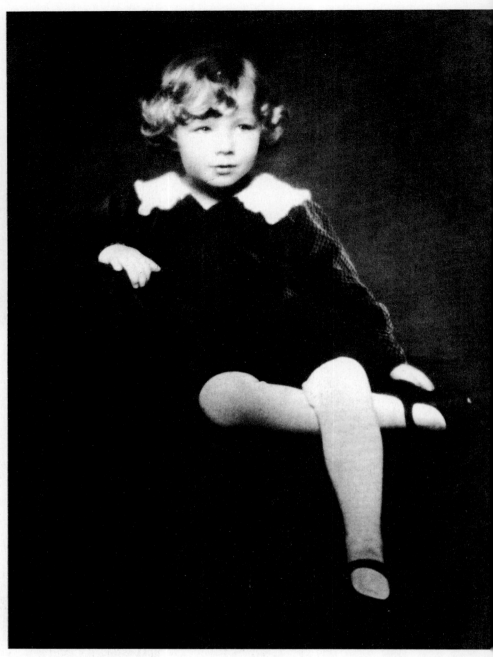

continued to function without interruption after the end of the war. Sons Max and Michael were in West Germany in 1946. Käthe Kruse followed in 1950 and Sofie in 1951. They immediately began to build new Käthe Kruse workshops. For more information, see page 36. Donauwörth became their new home. Kruse dolls are still manufactured there.

Today, this type of operation is extremely expensive because of the cost of hand labor. Plastic heads that are cheaper and easier to manufacture are used to help cut costs.

The Käthe Kruse dolls have lost a great deal of their individual original character as a result. But even today the painting of the eyes and mouth are done by hand. The human-hair wigs are knotted by hand and much of the clothing is sewn by hand.

Käthe Kruse's daughter, Johanna, expanded the production program. *Rumpumpel,* 13 inches (32cm) tall; *Mummelchen,* 14 inches (36cm) tall; and *Däumlinchen,* 10 inches (25cm) tall, are designated *Hanne Kruse Models.* Hanne was Johanna's nickname. The firm also successfully manufactures plush animals and plush balls.

Above: Film actress Agnes Countess of Esterhazy with Käthe Kruse's nursing care doll *Träumerchen.*

Left: Son Max, born in 1921, became the author of children's books. When he was still very small, he was affectionately referred to as Maxl-Baby. He was the inspiration for *Träumerchen.* Dr. Wagner, the family physician, gave Käthe Kruse the idea to design a doll to teach infant care.

Käthe Kruse was a pioneer in her life's work. She wrote, "The germ of my life's work comes from Max Kruse. The development is from me. In me, the idea of a doll was connected from the very beginning with the wish to produce a child for the child."

She was the mother in her business, not the boss. She always communicated a great deal of heart. She was a refreshing person who pursued her ideas with consistency and patience. Her greatest care was given to the craftsmanlike preparation of her doll children. "Only the hand can create what proceeds from the hand to the heart," she said.

This energetic and intelligent woman added something to the world of children, making doll collectors richer. When someone says, "It looks like a Käthe Kruse doll," to a charming doll, it is one of the greatest compliments for Käthe Kruse.

Käthe Kruse wrote about life and work. "Yes, I am the doll-Kruse. But I didn't invent anything and I didn't establish any workshop. I certainly never worked to earn money. Everything simply grew and cost me no special effort. Max planted the seed, telling me, 'make a doll,' and I simply pursued my own feelings.

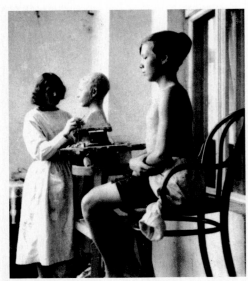
Daughter Sofie, born in 1904, was gifted. Here she sculpts her brother, Friedebald.

Above: Wax bust of Friedebald as it stands in Sofie's apartment. No doll was fashioned after this bust.

Above right: Friedebald, about 8 years old. His bust, modeled by Igor von Jakimow, was the prototype for *Doll VIII, The German Child.* It was called *Friedebald, Ilsebill, Susi, Veronika-Lolott, Ellen* and *Julchen.* They all have the same *Doll VIII* head.

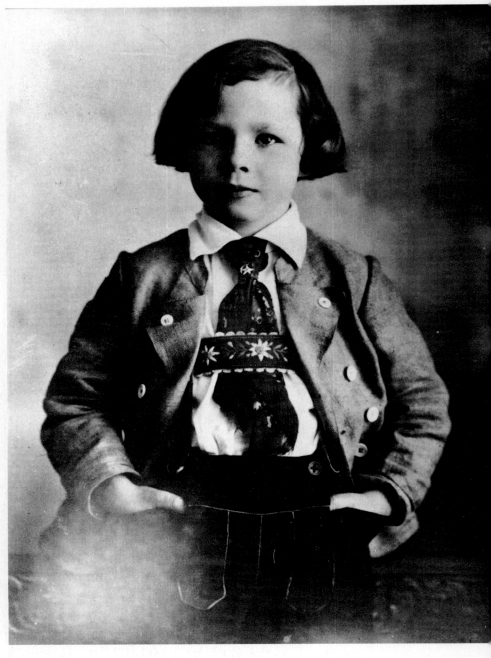

"No, I am not crazy about children. I am really only interested in humans. I love children to the extent that the human already evident in the child has charm for me. I don't love them because they are sweet and small because they grow to be pests and egoists. I could never tolerate quarrels. I've never been able to tolerate them, not even from my own children.

"I'm also not a philosopher, but perhaps a lively idealist. It is my conviction we come into the world furnished with certain gifts we can't change. To develop that which is good and to cultivate it and to improve that which is not so good as much as possible, this seems to me to be the basic task of all education."

Käthe Kruse remained a wife and mother even with her professional engagements and business duties. After three daughters, Maria in 1902, Sofie in 1904 and Johanna in 1909, she gave birth to four boys. They were Michael, nicknamed *Michel,* in 1911; Jochen, nicknamed *Jockerle,* in 1912; Friedebald, nicknamed *Friedel,* in 1918; and Max, nicknamed *Maxl,* in 1921. Their names were given to many dolls. The boys helped

Above: *Ilsebill in the Wind.* Jochen Kruse arranged and photographed this *Doll VIII.*

Left: *Doll VIII* as *Friedebald* and *Ilsebill* on a Christmas shopping trip. This doll came onto the market in 1929. It was 21 inches (52cm) tall and had a swivel head. The human-hair wig, knotted by hand, was new. In the Kruse brochures, many accessories were also offered that were not manufactured by the Kruse workshops.

build their mother's business and bring the Kruse dolls even more fame as they grew.

Life was not always easy for this beloved mother, emancipated wife and successful businesswoman. After more than 40 years of marriage, her husband and friend, Max Kruse, died at the age of 89 in 1942. His artistic works and inventions were respected and recognized. He never achieved the popularity of Käthe Kruse and her dolls, but he invented many things. These include a flying machine and a sculpture-copying machine. He owned several patents.

One of his inventions was a three-dimensional stage design called the *transparent stage sky.* He created the new stage for Max Reinhardt's production of *Salome* by Wilde on Sept. 21, 1902. He created the perspective of great distance using a curved horizon and by decreasing the size of background buildings. The footlights were eliminated. Instead, various colored spotlights of different intensities provided atmosphere in the room.

One year after this versatile thinker and artist died, his son Jochen

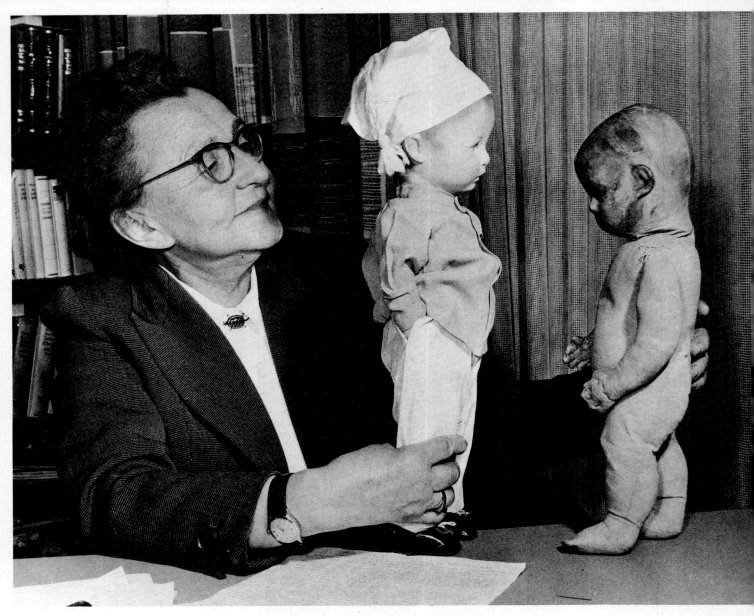

Käthe Kruse places an early *Doll I*, on the right, opposite a later edition.

died. It was the result of a head injury he had as a child. Käthe Kruse suffered terribly. A year later, a World War II accident killed her son, Friedebald.

She was tested by suffering but always filled with courage for life. Käthe Kruse celebrated her 80th birthday in 1963 with her children, grandchildren and great-grandchildren. In the last years of her life, Maria, her oldest daughter, lovingly cared for her. In the hospital at Murnau in upper Bavaria, shortly before her 85th birthday, quite silently her heart simply stopped beating. This is from an obituary by Sofie Rehbinder-Kruse. The life of a wonderful mother and wife came to an end. Käthe Kruse worked for beauty, whether acting, painting, in photography or her dolls. She unintentionally created a lasting monument and gave joy to millions of people.

Top left: *Sternschnuppchen,* which means *shooting star,* around 1932. It was 14 inches (35cm) tall, with the face of *Doll I.* Cloth bonnet formed the rear of the head and was sewn onto the face. Head was stuffed very softly. For Christmas, *Sternschnuppchen* wore a removable star on its head.

Center left: 10-inch (25cm) *Bambino* dolls, with removable wings. The head of *Doll I* was used for these dolls.

Left: Three Kruse grandchildren and a friend with a *Sternschnuppchen,* on the right, and a *Hampelchen.*

Top right: First Show-Window Doll from 1928. It was modeled after Friedebald's head and was the beginning of a new Show-Window Doll era for Kruse workshops.

Lower right: Japanese woman doll from *Marketplace in Permanbuko* for the Imperial Museum in Amsterdam. Head by Igor von Jakimow.

Käthe Kruse

München 13
Mittermayrstraße 10 ᴵᴵ
Telefon 37 34 03

29.9.58.

Geliebte freunde Alle!

Nein, es ist nicht möglich, jedem Einzelnen auch nur mit ein paar wenigen persönlichen Zeilen zu danken! Ich bin so zu-geschüttet worden mit Beweisen von Zuneigung und Freundschaft, — mit Briefen und Telegrammen und Karten, mit zarthaften Blumen und schönen Angebinden, daß ich eben einfach garnicht dazu kommen kann. Es war, und ist noch überwältigend! Aber seid unbesorgt, — ich bleibe bescheiden. — Nur echt recht! — Es war so schön, daß ich's erleben durfte. —

Ich bitte Euch, mit diesem kleinen herzlichen Dank fürlieb zu nehmen. — Ich wünsche Euch Allen etwas Schönes! —

Eure

Käthe Kruse

Käthe Kruse's handwritten letter thanking friends for flowers and congratulations on her 75th birthday.

34

Käthe Kruse, 81, photographed by grandson, Torsten Rehbinder, a professional photographer. He was attracted to photography like his mother, Sofie Rehbinder-Kruse, and his grandmother, Käthe Kruse.

Doll Types, Workshops and Manufacturing

Käthe Kruse Workshops

Käthe Kruse received her first order in the fall of 1911 for 150 dolls to be delivered to America. She had no suitable workshop and quickly decided to turn her Berlin apartment into one. The Kruses settled in Bad Kösen after searching for suitable rooms in a nice location. They rented a house in the new settlement Naumburg. They rented workrooms on another street. Käthe Kruse was expecting her fifth child, Jochen, who was born in December 1912.

Käthe Kruse dolls were largely manufactured by hand, so the Kruses didn't have to buy complicated machinery. Käthe Kruse dolls from Bad Kösen became treasured worldwide as a quality toy.

Käthe Kruse dolls continued to be manufactured for about 11 years in the same place. Then they began to look for a larger place in the same town. A school that was for sale met all their requirements. The Käthe Kruse workshops found its home there from 1922 until the end of World War II. The family then moved to West Germany.

Max Kruse, the son, began building new Kruse workshops in Bad Pyrmont in the spring of 1946. Dr. Michael Kruse, another son, did the same thing in Donauwörth, in December 1946. Both businesses were combined in February 1949 in Donauwörth, and both sons directed the business.

The firm was divided into Käthe Kruse Play Dolls Limited and Käthe Kruse Show-Window Figures Limited in December 1957 or January 1958. The Schildkröt firm owned 70% of Käthe Kruse Play Dolls Limited and Max Kruse owned 30%. In 1962, daughter Johanna Adler-Kruse took over her brother's 30% of the business. In 1977, her husband acquired the 70% of the business from Schildkröt, which had been making Celluloid Käthe Kruse dolls. Once again the business was 100% in the family.

Philosophy of Dolls to Play With

Käthe Kruse dolls are special because she designed dolls for children to play with. She meant for her dolls to be soft, warm and durable. As she said, "a child for the child."

She didn't want them to be as fragile as porcelain, as hard and stiff as wood, as light as Celluloid and as easily damaged as papier-mâché. The joints shouldn't squeak or crack and shouldn't be visible.

These ideas ripened in the 5 years between 1906 and 1910 when she made dolls for her children. She decided to produce dolls commercially after the surprising response to her dolls at the Berlin exhibition *Home-made Toys* in 1910. She was able to put her experience into practice. Her great success, which surprised many, was not luck. "I knew exactly how a doll had to be," she said.

She wanted to avoid the all-too-sweet cliché of porcelain-head puppets. She wanted her dolls to be primitive and natural. These criteria were realized best in her dolls. This explains the success secret of Käthe Kruse dolls.

Rented private villa in Bad Kösen was first workshop in 1912. Käthe Kruse begins final inspection in exhibition room.

Far left: Second house from front is first workshop of Käthe Kruse dolls. It was in Bad Kösen.

Left: Old school building in Bad Kösen was bought at the end of 1927. Käthe Kruse dolls were manufactured here until after World War II.

Artistic Production

Käthe Kruse had a strong sense of quality. She was a part of the business from the beginning. She was a co-worker who improved and checked quality. Her dolls were quality products because of their artistic production.

Each doll had its own personality because it was painted by hand, and each doll was a bit different. Manufacture of the dolls was so costly and time-consuming that, even 70 years ago, not every household could afford one.

Käthe Kruse continued the handwork of her dolls for many decades. She rejected machine manufacturing as energetically as she rejected painting with stencils.

Käthe Kruse never got rich despite the worldwide reputation of her dolls. Not many dolls could be manufactured by the Kruse workshops in Bad Kösen on this artisan basis. Many more bisque porcelain-head dolls could be made because of production methods. Hundreds of thousands, even millions, of these can be made in a year. Many of these dolls made in Germany and France are available today in great numbers for collectors. Kruse dolls had one manufacturer, the Kruse workshops. It's still a middle-class enterprise that prepares about 15,000 dolls each year.

The Kruse workshops in Donauwörth do about the same amount, or less, of business as they did in Bad Kösen, although they have adopted modern production methods and materials.

Confusion of Names and Types

The first Käthe Kruse doll came out in 1911. It had no siblings until about 1922. It had an unimaginative name but became a star. It later was called *Doll I* and that name remained.

Doll I embodied a new doll type. It had a cloth head, painted hair and costly worked-cloth body that was 17 inches (43cm) tall. *Doll I* was dressed as a boy or girl with no change in the face. It was carried in the catalog with various names.

Imaginative clothing was added for exhibitions in later years, instead of developing new doll types. The dolls received names depending on their clothing, which distinguished them in the catalog. Many collectors believe there are 30 to 40 types of dolls and are surprised to learn there is only one. Dolls resemble each other the way one egg resembles another, so this mistake is understandable.

Each doll was visually different because of clothing and hand painting. Different wigs in later years distinguished the dolls. They turned out a little different each time because the facial color could be light or dark. The eyes or mouth could be larger or smaller. Sometimes the child had red cheeks and at other times it looked delicate and pale. Variations also occurred because the head could be slightly different because it was stuffed by hand.

The worldwide fame of the Käthe Kruse dolls began with this doll. *Schlenkerchen, Doll II,* expanded the Kruse offerings in 1922. See pages 74 to 75 for more information. *Doll I* continued to be produced until about 1952. It had a human-hair wig under the designation *I H.* The small, 14-inch (35cm) *Inexpensive Kathe Kruse Doll* was introduced in 1927. It was developed because of inflation. It is a smaller version of the popular *Doll I.*

Käthe Kruse introduced new doll types with *Dolls V and VI, Traumerchen* and *Du Mein,* and *Doll VIII, Friedebald* and *The German Child.*

Käthe Kruse, standing by the shelves, gives a final inspection to dolls prepared for shipping at Bad Kösen workshops.

Left: Arrangements of *Doll I* from 1911.

39

Above: Painting hair required skilled hands. Oil paints were used so dolls could be washed.

Opposite page, top: Sewing room in Bad Kösen workshops. Fur-sewing machines were used to sew bodies.

Opposite page, bottom: Smoothing and applying the layers of color to cloth heads.

These created excitement and are still loved by children and collectors.

The blond and brown human-hair wigs used beginning in 1929 were especially responsible for *Doll VIII's* success.

These five doll types and a variety of names caused lots of confusion. This makes it difficult for everyone who first deals with the dolls.

Käthe Kruse gave a literary touch to this in the 1930s. She wrote *Kuddelmuddel*, a lively children's book. See pages 124 to 127 for more information. *Kuddelmuddel* means confusion. The book deals primarily with the Kruse Show-Window Dolls. It seems obvious she wanted to solve some of the misunderstandings with *Kuddelmuddel*.

This book is designed to help the collector understand the five doll types. The chart on pages 64 to 65 gives an overview of the doll versions manufactured from 1910-1952. This provides facts about size, dates and other characteristics. It took almost 2 years to collect the information.

Käthe Kruse Dolls: Identification with Her Children?

We often hear and read that Käthe Kruse's children were the models for her dolls.

Her husband invented the manufacturing technique for the heads. He molded the first forms with his sensitive artist's hands.

The model for *Doll I* wasn't Maria or Sofie. Käthe Kruse bought a head by a Flemish artist that reminded her of her daughters. She told Sofie this Flemish head was the model for *Doll I*.

Her son, Max, was the inspiration for *Schlenkerchen* and *Träumerchen*. Käthe Kruse describes *Träumerchen's* development in a charming story on page 125.

Her son, Friedebald, was the first and probably the only real model. He was especially charming as a child. In this family of artists he was chosen again and again as a model.

Max Kruse's son-in-law, Igor von Jakimow, sculpted a bust of Friedebald in 1921. This bust is the original head for *Dolls VIII* and *IX* and a Show-Window Doll. Seeing one of these dolls gives the impression of seeing Freidebald alive. There is an example on page 112.

Sofie created most of the Show-Window Doll heads. She used her brother Friedebald and her other siblings as models. Later she used her children. The dolls are pictured on pages 60 to 61.

An expressive bust of 19-year-old Friedebald was the only one of her works she could take with her from Bad Kösen. It stands today in her apartment. A picture of the bust is on page 30. Friedebald has been immortalized in a generation of dolls despite his death at a young age.

Max Kruse sculpted a wood bust of his daughter, Maria, in 1908. This was later purchased by the city of Berlin. No doll head was ever developed from this bust.

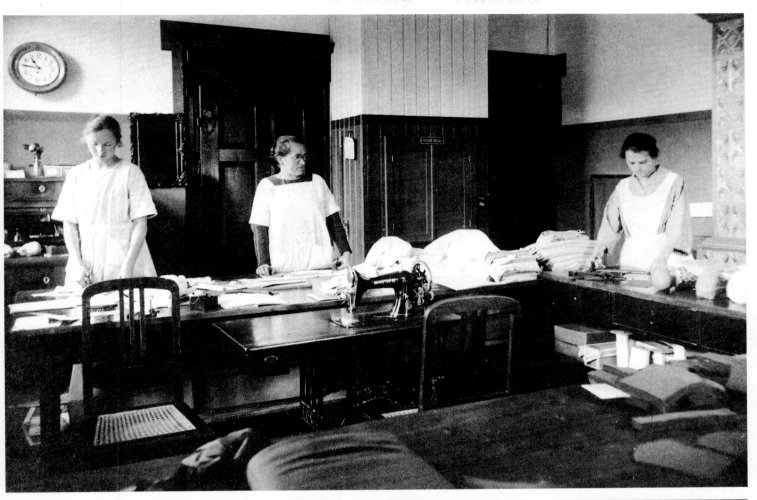

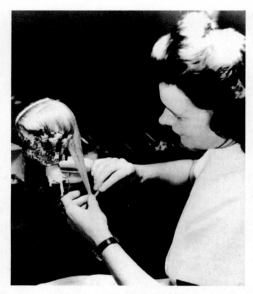

Above: After knotting wigs, curls were applied.

Opposite page, top: Mouths, cheeks and nostrils were painted after priming.

Opposite page, bottom: Specialists were required to paint the eyes.

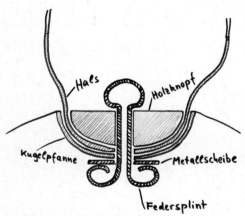

Schematic drawing by Udo Körle, showing how Käthe Kruse doll heads swiveled. Cotter pin was pushed through half-circle of wood in the head.

Anatomy of Käthe Kruse Dolls
Cloth, Magnesite, Cardboard and Plastic Dolls

In the beginning Kruse made only cloth heads. The adult Show-Window Dolls used magnesite for functional reasons beginning in 1933. It was used in *Träumerchen* and *Du Mein* around 1937.

Swivel heads for play dolls were molded from cardboard after World War II in Bad Kösen and Donauwörth. They were covered with cloth and have a seam in the back. Firmly attached cloth heads were prepared according to the traditional method at the same time. Plastic heads have been used since 1952 because they are less expensive.

Firmly Attached Heads and Swivel Heads

Käthe Kruse dolls all had firmly attached heads until 1928. *Doll VIII, The German Child*, introduced the swivel head in 1929.

All dolls with a firmly attached head were stuffed. All swivel heads were molded and were usually hollow. When they were stuffed, the stuffing was light to allow the swivel mechanism to move. The drawing at lower left shows how swivel heads were attached with a cotter pin.

Producing the Head

The head is always the most important detail of a doll. It was Käthe Kruse's job to make the head delightful to look at and easy to play with. Studying an old *Doll I* shows what this means. The face half, also called the *face mask*, is relatively stable and firm and does not feel hard.

The back of the head and neck were sewn onto the face mask. The back of the head feels soft even though the head was firmly stuffed.

A positive and negative bronze form, with a space of about 1mm, was used to prepare the face. The sewn face mask with the neck and back of the head were made of flesh-colored nettle cloth. These were stretched over the positive form and firmly pressed by hand into the negative form.

This resulted in a soft preforming of the face that was further sculpted with warm wax into the negative form. This wax was made of many ingredients. The most important was collodiom, which made it harder and less heat sensitive.

A preformed, small metal nose was added to the head. This nettle-cloth-and-wax mask was strengthened with glue-soaked gauze. Head cloths, also called *pate cloths*, were sewn together when they were hard and dry. This was formed into a head with fine wood shavings and deer hair.

Doll I had three pate seams for many years because it was stuffed by hand. This helps collectors recognize a *Doll I* head but doesn't prove they are dealing with an early doll. Several other criteria are used, such as the type of painting, shape of the body, size of hips or if it had sewn-on thumbs.

The expensive process of molding the face and hand stuffing the head was later changed. The negative form was lined with three layers of moist gauze then molded by machine. It was removed from the negative form, turned inside out over the positive, and the edges trimmed.

The nettle face was turned inside out and molded onto the gauze mask in the machine. After the molded back half had been glued, both back flaps were sewn together.

Above: Sofie with an armful of dolls needing repairs. She was active in her mother's shop from childhood.

Opposite page, top: Rosinchen the donkey, with Sicilian cart. For many years he took doll packages to Bad Kösen post office.

Opposite page, bottom: Sofie at the wheel of Buick purchased in the 1930s. Next to her is her mother, Käthe Kruse. Behind them, Friedebald, Max, Johanna, Michael and Jochen.

Stuffed, firmly attached heads always have three pate seams. Swivel heads with cloth coverings always have one seam running down the pate. Plastic heads, used since 1952, have no seams.

Head patterns hand-designed by Käthe Kruse are published here for the first time. One part is shown on page 100. We also show the body pattern of Nov. 7, 1911, for the first time on the same page.

The oldest *Doll I* examples were manufactured by Kämmer & Reinhardt for a few months in 1911. This firm did not use the expensive process of head production described above. They needed to work more easily, more quickly and with less cost to be efficient. They used two firm spheres for the face and back of the head, which were then joined together. These don't have the typical soft back of the head. These dolls are rare. For more information, see pages 66 to 67.

Painting the Head

All Käthe Kruse doll heads were hand-painted until 1952, and the dolls became individuals. Oil paints were used so the dolls could be washed.

A palette knife was used for the first coat. The second primer was then applied. After each painting, the head was sanded smooth.

The third and final painting used gentle brushstrokes in the still-wet paint. This produced the cheeks and hair. The wet-on-wet painting technique was important because it was the only way to make delicate children's hair. After drying, the eyes and mouth were applied as the final stage.

Each face turned out differently because of hand-painting. Some doll faces had delicate, light paint and some had strong colors. Early dolls sometimes show thin paint or heavy wear, allowing the structure of the face to show through. That is not a problem! The doll's charm is increased because of this. These dolls are especially loved by collectors.

Eyes

Käthe Kruse dolls have painted eyes except for Celluloid dolls, which were produced with glass or plastic eyes for a few months. The eyebrows were delicately indicated. Eyelashes were not painted except for *Schlenkerchen*, which had open eyes with lashes, and *Träumerchen*, which had closed eyes with lashes.

The early *Doll I* had almost exclusively a painted, radiating iris. This appears in individual cases in the 1940s in *Doll I H, Dolls VIII, X and XII.*

Käthe Kruse took the greatest pains with eye painting. This difficult labor was reserved for a few specialists. Transfer pictures and other methods were easier, but were rejected as unsatisfactory.

Mouth

The mouth of the Käthe Kruse doll is almost always closed. Only *Schlenkerchen*, with its smiling face, had an open-closed mouth. An example is shown on page 74.

An unusual style was preferred for painting the mouth. This is a characteristic facial expression of Käthe Kruse dolls. The upper lip is painted in a single drawn bow showing no depression in the middle.

Käthe Kruse

Bewegungsbeispiele zu Blatt 3 und 6

PUPPE XII "Hampelchen"
45 cm groß, mit lockeren Beinchen;
die ideale Puppe für das Kleinkind

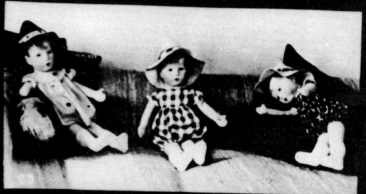

durch eine Knopfvorrichtung im Rücken kann es auch *frei* stehen,

beim Sitzen oder Liegen oder Hängen aber

nehmen seine lockeren

Beinchen immer

natürliche Stellungen ein,

während Beinchen mit Scheibengelenken zwar gerade und fest stehen können, -- beim Sitzen oder Liegen aber spreizen müssen

Above: *Doll I* as streetcar conductor on post card from Jan. 30, 1918.

Opposite page: Photo was taken around 1938 in Bad Kösen. It shows a worker holding a *Friedebald*. On the top row stand *Doll VIIIs*, with examples of *Doll VII*. On lower shelf are *Hampelchen*, *Doll XII*, 18-inch and 14-inch (45cm and 35cm) sizes without wigs. *Doll VIII*, *German Child*, got its name when the workshops got an order to set up three-dimensional scenes with dolls symbolizing the European child. Four of these three-dimensional scenes were developed from paintings. *The Daughter of Roberto Strozzi*, by Titian, was used for the Italian child. The Spanish child was modeled after *The Infantine Margarethe* by Velazquez. *The Age of Innocence* by Reynolds was the model for the English child. The German child was modeled after *The Daughter of the Painter* by Hübner. *Doll VIII* became known as *The German Child.*

Crudely sewn-on fingers of *Doll I* around 1910-1912, gave the impression of *frog's hands*. Hands were further refined in 1913.

Doll II, *Schlenkerchen*, had a chubby body covered with cloth and loosely sewn-on head. Instead of nettle cloth, a soft, elastic tricot material was used. An example is shown on page 103. Dolls covered with tricot also had a tricot-covered head. Examples include *Schlenkerchen*, *Träumerchen* and *Du Mein*. The open mouth prevented using nettle cloth on *Schlenkerchen's* head.

Schlenkerchen was charming to look at even when it was naked because it was not deformed by visible joints. The Little Soldier was the model for the body. It was produced according to a new industrial technique. Fine, thin, bundled wires reaching into the hands and feet formed the inner structure of the doll. Solid metal rods or tubes replaced bones and allowed joints to move freely and guaranteed greatest mobility. The upper and lower body was separated by two metal plates, which allowed the waist to move.

The skeleton was covered with cotton batting and wrapped with gauze or narrow cloth bands. The body was covered with Egyptian tricot. This made the small body warm and soft as well as movable. *Doll II* wasn't up to heavy use during play because the Egyptian tricot broke down quickly through contact with the wire skeleton.

Träumerchen, *Doll V*, was first produced in 1923. It was available at first only with closed eyes. Again, body construction was different. The doll was called *Sandbaby* because little bags of sand were distributed in the body to give the doll the weight of a genuine baby. It also felt like a real baby when it was held. Sand bags were later replaced by lead weights.

The same baby with open eyes was called *Du Mein*. *Träumerchen* and *Du Mein* became very popular. Two versions were made to meet market demand.

The body in Model A had a colored tricot suit. Model B had a nettle-cloth body stuffed with deer or reindeer hair like other Käthe Kruse dolls. More information is found on page 76. Model A was manufactured with a movable skeleton like *Schlenkerchen*.

Doll VIII, *Friedebald*, also called *The German Child*, appeared in 1929. It caused excitement because of its stately 21-inch (52cm) size. This doll was large and slender compared to the previous little, compact Käthe Kruse dolls with wide hips.

Its slim legs no longer had five seams. It had one vertical seam in the back and a cross seam at the knee. The body had three seams instead of eight. Legs were attached with disc joints like *Doll I*.

The German Child was produced 4 years before Hitler took office. Käthe Kruse was criticized after 1945 because of its name. In answer, she wrote, "Many persons thought ill of us because this doll bore the name *The German Child*. I cannot understand why Germans would consider the word German offensive and it was indeed never intended to be anything political. The English understood it much better than my German opponents. They called this new doll *Faithful Child*."

Doll IX, *The Little German Child*, came onto the market at the same time. It was 14 inches (35cm) tall.

Doll XII, *Hampelchen*, had loosely attached arms and legs.

Christmas post card from Dec. 23, 1917. Santa brought a Käthe Kruse *Doll I.*

How to Recognize Käthe Kruse Dolls

Markings

A running number was stamped with paint on the left sole of genuine Käthe Kruse dolls. The original Käthe Kruse signature was on the left sole. Dolls had a tag with the trademark on their wrists until 1928.

The doll carried a tag with the name Käthe Kruse around its neck beginning in 1929. The marking on the foot remained the same. The doll's catalog name was sometimes printed on the tag or marked by hand.

Made in Germany, U.S. Zone was printed on the tag beginning in 1947. This continued until 1949 or 1951, according to the company's brochure. This text was stamped on the right sole along with the number.

After Käthe Kruse moved to West Germany in 1951, the same dolls continued to be manufactured for a few years in East Germany. They were marked with a triangular stamp saying *VEB* on the right sole. On the left, the number and *VEB, Bad Kösen a.d. Saale* were marked. The original Käthe Kruse signature is missing from *VEB* dolls.

The trademark shield around the neck, the number and the name on the left sole are marked on dolls manufactured today. The tag is often missing because it is thrown away after the doll is purchased.

The name and number stamped on the foot is sometimes unreadable. Washing the doll or frequent playing makes the stamp illegible or disappear. For these reasons, you often have to know these dolls to identify them. Käthe Kruse dolls are usually easy to recognize because of their expressions. An exception is the Bing Dolls, page 111, that imitated Käthe Kruse dolls.

Numbering

All Käthe Kruse dolls have a number stamped on their left sole. Many collectors believe the numbers began with 1 and have continued. They think the doll's age can be learned from this.

This is not the case. Brochures from 1929-1930 seem to confirm this error by stating, "Only those are real Käthe Kruse dolls that bear on their left sole the name and the running number."

According to Sofie Rehbinder-Kruse, the company used a system of serial numbers for checking, repairing and reclaiming the dolls. Within different series, numbers are continuous.

Sometimes dolls were coded for business purposes. This occurred at least when home laborers were employed. Then the company could identify the makers by their numbers in case of complaints. Running numbers were *never* used continuously from the beginning. The numbering-system documents were lost when the company moved from Bad Kösen to Donauwörth.

Identification by Size

A doll's size helps determine the age of a Käthe Kruse doll by identifying the doll type. For example, if a 21-inch (52cm) doll is reported to be made before 1920, it can't be true. Käthe Kruse dolls 21 inches tall were first produced in 1929.

This doll could be from any number of years. Until 1922, only *Doll I* was made and it was 17 inches (43cm) tall. *Schlenkerchen* was made in 1922. It had a smiling face and introduced the 13-inch (33cm) size.

The table on pages 64 and 65 contains the sizes of various Käthe Kruse dolls.

Identification by Painting

Käthe Kruse dolls only had painted hair until 1928. Käthe Kruse dolls with wigs came out in 1929. *Dolls I* and *II* still had painted hair after that year. A *Doll I* of the Kruse doll family is not necessarily very old just because it has painted hair. It could have been made at almost any time. Some dolls are still manufactured with painted hair. This only occurs on plastic heads.

If a *Doll I* with painted hair also has a separate sewn-on thumb and very wide hips, it is a very old *Doll I* from as far back as 1913. See pages 102 and 103 for examples. A *Doll I* can even be older, from 1911-12, if it has simple sewn-on fingers that look like frogs' hands. For more information, see page 66.

The radiating iris of the eyes can help determine age. It was painted on some dolls until the 1930s. In individual cases, it was done even later.

Identification by Head Seam

An early *Doll I* head with painted hair had three pate seams. A smaller version of *Doll I*, the *Doll VII*, came on the market in 1927. It had painted hair and three pate seams. *Doll VII* with Head V, *Du Mein*, has three pate seams. See page 83.

There was a third version of *Doll I* with three seams. This was *Doll I H* with a human-hair wig. The *H* stands for hair.

Doll X with Head I had a swivel head with one seam.

Cardboard heads had a cloth cover and one seam.

Doll II, *Schlenkerchen*, was manufactured only with painted hair. It had one seam running down the back of the head.

One pate seam was necessary for dolls molded by machine. These began in 1929 with *Doll VIII*, *Friedebald*, which had a wig. For many dolls, hand stuffing was continued. *Dolls I H* and *XII* are examples.

Dolls with firmly attached heads had three seams. Dolls with swivel heads had one seam, as a general rule.

Beginning in 1952, there was no seam because heads were made of plastic. Of most value to collectors are the heads made of cloth by hand with one or three seams. When purchasing a Käthe Kruse doll with a wig, look for the seam at the back of the head. You might have to raise the wig a little off the neck. Be sure to check with the seller before doing that.

Kruse grandchildren, Sofie's children, under Christmas tree with *Träumerchen*.

Show-Window Dolls were manufactured in adult sizes beginning in 1933. Show-window figure, *Elisabeth,* dressed by son, Jochen, in Michael's Berlin silk shop. Jochen composed the photograph.

Above: Show-window figures *Elisabeth* and *Hoffmann* in elegant dress. Sofie's tennis teacher in Ascona was model for *Hoffmann.*

Opposite page: Sofie Kruse appears to converse with her show-window figure, *Margarete,* at Leipzig Fair in 1935.

Käthe Kruse Show-Window Figures
By Sofie Rehbinder-Kruse

Helping to write a book about the old Käthe Kruse play dolls is a wonderful task full of memories for me. Lydia Richter asked me to describe Show-Window Dolls because they were part of my mother's work. Show-Window Dolls were very similar to mannequins, but their design was more refined.

The public and window dressers became attached to the children's figures. They became children "who spoke to the heart, who reminded one of children and wore their clothes." They wore clothes to sell them.

I constructed the ball-jointed skeletons in those days with the help of our plumber. I gave my mother, on her 50th birthday in 1933, the first doll of this type. I had modeled the head from a magazine photo of the charming actress Liane Haid.

Development of these dolls took a long time, and it was even longer before Käthe Kruse figures conquered show windows. We began preparing for this with the Little Soldiers, the Doll-Room Dolls, *Schlenkerchen,* *Träumerchen* and *Du Mein.* Designing these dolls helped develop a wire skeleton with movable limbs.

The Oberpollinger Department Store of Munich asked us to make our play dolls life-size for a Mother's Day window. The idea was a challenge to us. It was like asking a coachmaker to build an automobile. Entire worlds lie between one and the other.

To make them we had to use a modification of the existing skeleton. The doll had to be able to stand, and bones had to be firm. A new, unsuspected problem developed. We needed lots of heads. I had to sculpt and develop my talent. Each clothing size needed at least three heads. I had an unending need for models. I began with my younger siblings, with their friends, then with my friends. This didn't make me exactly popular. Everybody warned everyone else of the unavoidable sitting ceremonies.

Heads of Show-Window Dolls could no longer be manufactured in jute or gauze with a nettle-cloth cover. The forms would have been much too heavy and clumsy. They were laminated out of various layers of smooth and coarse materials soaked in magnesite.

The Show-Window Doll heads had to be interchangable. Whatever expression it was supposed to convey—joy or thoughtfulness—had to be transmitted by the head. In the case of child figures, we had to show with the head whether it was a boy or girl.

The head also had to be movable. It had to turn and move up and down. To prevent heads from getting on wrong-size bodies, each size had to have a different four-cornered pin beneath the head. This furnished a stable connection to the body.

The figures had to have hand-knotted, human-hair wigs. Wigs had to be interchangable and removable to be washed and curled. Whether the wig was blond or brown, long or short, curls or braids, it had to express what was needed.

The problems and experiments were endless. Despite the problems, the first figures in Oberpollinger's window were attractive. Other businesses requested more in different sizes with other heads or with other hairstyles. The artistic arrangements of the Show-Window Dolls were created by my brother, Jochen. He died young and left no successor. His taste, his ability and his love for this work contributed so much.

A mother had to be added to the show-window children. This became the first ball-jointed doll with Liane Haid's head. It took 5 years from the

Max Kruse created a bust of **Show-Window Doll Eva**, shown here with Sofie. Sofie created head of Show-Window Doll in flowered dress. *Margarete*, modeled after Liane Haid, served as Show-Window Doll mother.

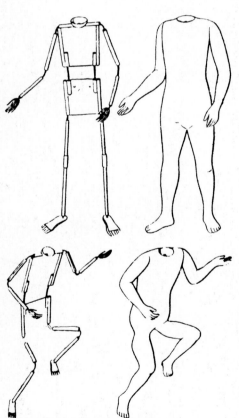

Above: These skeletons are for Show-Window Figure A that could stand, sit or lie. Durable, flexible skeleton was made of thin wire bundles and metal supports. Body was shaped by hand, stuffed with cellulose and covered with non-fading tricot.

Opposite page, top right: The Kruse family making dolls as a team in 1934.

development of Show-Window Dolls in children's sizes using the modified skeleton to the ball-jointed dolls for the adult size.

I wanted to make a small contribution on this subject with these remarks.

Sofie Rehbinder-Kruse

New Show-Window Culture for the Fashion Industry

More doll heads for Show-Window Dolls were available than for children's dolls. Each head could be used several ways. It could be a boy or girl. They could be changed further by using different wigs. Dolls were also characterized by various names and order numbers. More than 90 show-window heads were offered for children's sizes up to 14. All are pictured on pages 60 and 61. In addition, there were many adult sizes.

These dolls revolutionized German and European show windows within a few years. Existing mannequins did not look as natural as Kruse dolls. Kruse dolls resembled humans because of the ability to move them and place them in different poses.

Figures being used until then resembled clothing stands. Kruse figures, according to a brochure, gave a "graceful representation of a natural person." Display windows presented goods for sale. The term *stacked window* in use at that time demonstrates this. The show window became a method of advertising with Kruse figures. It enticed shoppers to want the goods.

Window dressers and school classes created artistic show-window scenes and imaginative fairy-tale scenes with the movable Kruse figures. A new show-window culture had begun and Käthe Kruse had the lion's share. Her figures took a decisive role in the development of Show-Window Dolls.

Types of Show-Window Doll Bodies

The size of the Show-Window Dolls corresponded with clothing sizes of the fashion industry. Three basic types of figures in different sizes and mobility were developed. They were Figures A, B and C.

FIGURE A

There were two models of Figure A. One model could lie or sit and came in sizes 0 to 1. The other model could also stand when made in size 2. The body was modeled by hand out of cellulose and gauze bandages over a strong, bendable skeleton. The skeleton was made of bundles of thin wires and metal supports. The knee position couldn't be changed in either model.

Small step and spread positions could be created. The sitting legs on the size 0 to 1 could be adjusted to hang, rest on a surface or cross.

The upper body was flexible. The shoulders, elbows and hands were movable. Fingers and wrists could assume all positions.

The skin-colored covering of stretchable, light tricot could be cleaned and renovated.

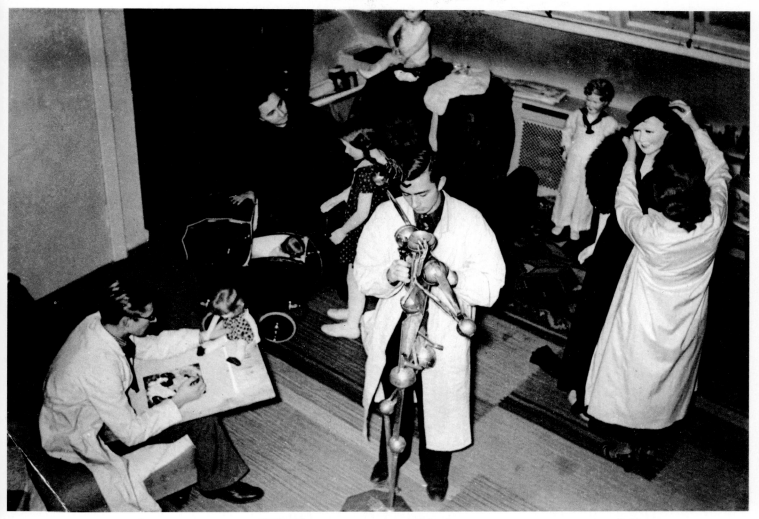

Jochen   **Käthe Kruse**   **Michael**   **Sofie**

Above: *Erich* in chic travel clothing of the 1930s with wide-cut pants, dust coat, cap and gaiters.

Left: Son Friedebald in 1934 with Show-Window Doll *Evchen*.

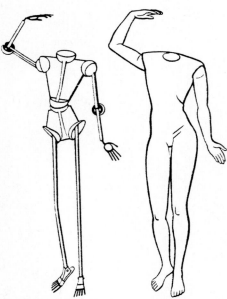

Above: Figure B had five ball-joints—one in middle of the body, two in shoulders and two in elbows. Leg position stayed the same while the upper body could have many positions.

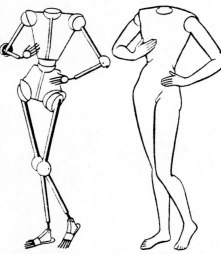

Above: Figure C had six additional ball-joints—two in hips, two in knees, two in knuckles. This permitted many positions of standing, sitting, kneeling and reclining.

FIGURE B

Figure B began with size 3. It could only stand. The upper body used five ball-joints to move. One was in the center of the body, two in the shoulders and two in the elbows. It could be turned and bent easily. Arms could be raised and lowered, and the elbows could be positioned in a variety of angles. See illustration at left.

FIGURE C

These were universal figures for teenagers and adults that could stand, sit and lie. Their 11 ball-joints made most human positions possible. See illustration at left.

The bodies of Figures B and C were manufactured like Figure A. Beginning in 1939, fingers were sewn separately.

All figures were able to stand alone. A pin stand was recommended to keep them standing securely. This could be ordered from the Kruse workshops. The ankle could be raised or lowered. It could be rotated and high-button shoes would fit on it. A hole in the sole of the foot was used to push the pin stand into the leg.

The children's sizes are listed in the following table. The size is always measured to the top of the head.

0 = 6 months	7 = 48 inches (120cm)
1 = 9 months	8 = 52 inches (130cm) (ages 7-8)
2 = 30 inches (75cm)	9 = 54 inches (135cm) (ages 9-10)
3 = 34 inches (85cm)	10 = 56 inches (140cm) (ages 9-10)
4 = 37 inches (92cm)	11 = 58 inches (145cm)
5 = 40 inches (100cm)	12 = 60 inches (150cm)
5K = 46 inches (116cm) (boy's size)	13 = 62 inches (155cm)
6 = 44 inches (110cm)	14 = 64 inches (160cm)

Beginning with size 9, figures were delivered in models B and C. The larger limbs kept the skeleton from being as flexible.

TEENAGERS

Size 36 = 41 inches (103cm)
Size 38 = 42 inches (106cm)
Names included *Marietta, Paola, Sybil, Julia, Ursel, Carina* and *Cornelia*.

WOMEN'S FIGURES

Size 38 = 66 inches (165cm)
Size 40 = 67 inches (168cm)
Size 42 = 68 inches (171cm)
Names included *Margarete, Elisabeth, Maria*.

MEN'S FIGURES

Sizes 44-50
Preferred size 48 = 72 inches (179cm)
Names included *Mr. Klug, Mr. Schnell*.
Sizes of 73 inches to 76 inches (182-190cm) were also available.

Donauwörth Show-Window Dolls

Show-Window Doll production began in Bad Kösen in 1928. It was continued after World War II in Donauwörth. Beginning in 1952, bodies were made of plastic over a metal skeleton and were covered with fade-proof tricot.

Heads of Show-Window Dolls

Heads could be moved freely, placed in any position and put on a variety of bodies within certain sizes. Heads could be ordered individually—each figure usually had three heads.

Käthe Kruse VERSTELLBARE SCHAUFENSTERFIGUREN

Show-Window Dolls costumed from four centuries in Fountainfest festival parade in Bad Kösen. Top left head is *Ilse*, rest are *Friedebald*.

Wigs were knotted of permanent-waved human hair. They were easy to curl and could be washed. Wigs could be removed by pressing two buttons on the temples. Wigs were interchangable, providing many variations. For example, with two bodies of the same size, a standing boy could be made out of a sitting girl.

The figures in each size were basically the same. They could be placed in a variety of positions depending on what they were supposed to be doing. More variety was possible by using wigs and heads within the sizes.

Top left: Grandson Torsten with his "twin" Show-Window Doll.

Top right: Granddaughter Angela.

Bottom left: Granddaughter Gundula, each with their twin Show-Window Dolls. All are children of Sofie Rehbinder-Kruse.

Above: Sofie works on a bust.

Show-Window Dolls in Child Sizes
Available sizes are listed in parentheses.

Renatchen (0)

Renatchen (1)

Mausel (2-3)

Mücke (2-3)

Mücke (2-3)

Mücke (2-3)

Jojo (2-3)

Reselind (2-3)

Mausel-Gudrun (2-3)

Friedebald (4-6)

Friedebald-Billy (4-6)

Niki (4-6)

Otto (4-6)

Frechdachs (4-6)

Friedl-Marlene (4-6)

Friedl-Philine (4-6)

Friedl-Regine (4-6)

Friedl-Karin (4-6)

Carola-Bärbel (4-6)

Carola-Heidi (4-6)

Carola-Marlene (4-6)

Carola-Ruth (4-6)

Carola-Hannerle (4-6)

Nina-Sonja (4-6)

Nina-Helga (4-6)

Nina-Wanda (4-6)

Nina-Gitta (4-6)

Susi-Gitta (5-6)

Susi-Ruth (5-6)

Susi-Heidi (5-6)

Susi-Wanda (5-6)

Susi-Regine (5-6)

Mimerle-Philine (5-6)

Mimerle-Helga (5-6)

Mimerle-Ruth (5-6)

Mimerle-Wanda (5-6)

Billy (5-6)

Mäxchen (5-6)

Seppl (6-9)

Erich (6-9)

Ilse-Theresli (6-9)

Ilschen (6-9)

Ilse-Margot (6-9)

Ilse-Hannerle (6-9)

Ilse-Bärbel (6-9)

Ilse-Karin (6-9)

Ilse-Dorle (6-9)

Lore-Philine (7)

Lore-Theresli (7)

Lore-Marlene (7)	Friedebald (7)	Nikolaus (7)	Nana-Gisela (7)	Nana-Erna (7)	Nana-Marlene (7)	Andreas (8-10)

Bernhard (8-10)	Angela-Sofie (8-10)	Angela-Philine (8-10)	Angela-Sabine (8-10)	Angela-Bärbel (8-10)	Angela-Marlene (8-10)	Birgit-Uschi (8-10)

Birgit-Philine (8-10)	Peter (10-12)	Peter-Billy (10-12)	Joachim (10-12)	Eva-Wanda (10-12)	Eva-Beate (10-12)	Eva-Dorette (10-12)

Eva-Philine (10-12)	Eva-Marlene (10-12)	Eva Barbel (10-12)	Karl (12-13)	Hans (12-13)	Karl-Billy (12-13)	Maria-Wanda (12-13)

Maria-Beate (12-13)	Maria-Margot (12-13)	Gretl-Dorette (12-13)	Gretl-Hilde (12-13)	Gretl-Susann (12-13)	Kai (14)	Julius (14)

Ursula-Susann (14)	Ursula-Wanda (14)	Ursula-Isolde (14)

Show-Window Dolls in children's sizes are of special interest to collectors. The heads were made of magnesite. Ninety child show-window figure heads were offered. There were actually 30 head types, because a different wig could make the head a boy or girl. This practice didn't work for teenager and adult dolls. Wigs with varying styles and colors could change the figure, but they always stayed male or female. Faces were too distinctive to exchange heads. About 100 head types, including child and adult heads, were produced in the 30 years they were manufactured.

Julia-Astrid (14)	Julia-Isolde (14)	Julia-Susann (14)

PUPPE VIII
DAS DEUTSCHE KIND
52 cm

201 Friedebald in einem neuen Joppenanzug rot · schwarz kariert, helle Hose mit Taschen, seidenes Sporthemd mit Schnalle am Hals, Leder-Gürtel und Sandalen . . RM 49.50 ungekleidet als Hosenmatz . RM 36.50

202 Annemarie aus Süddeutschland, trägt zum grün-weiß karierten Waschkleid mit rot · schwarz · weiß streifigem Jäckchen helle Lederschuhe . . . . RM 48.50 Kränzchen außerdem RM 1.25 ein Blumenkörbchen . RM 1.25 ungekleidet . . . RM 39.—

203 Florian in den Ferien, trägt ein helles Leinenhöschen, (gefüttert, mit Taschen), ein streifiges Vistra Hemd mit Schnallenschluß und helle Lederschuhe RM 46.— ungekleidet als Hosenmatz . . RM 36.50

204 Leonore im Frühlingskleidchen aus zartkarierter heller Bembergseide, mit Knöpfchen- und Kragenverzierungen, und weißen Schnallenschuhen RM 44.50 dieselbe ungekleidet RM 36.—

205 Veronika in Organdy, hellblumig mit schmalem blauen Samtband · Ausputz, weißem Batistunterkleidchen und Schnallenschuhen . . . RM 42.— dieselbe Puppe als Hemdenmatz . . RM 33.

206 S im rot gette K gengarn Ledersch Kränzche die Pup

PUPPE I
MIT GEMALTEN
HÄRCHEN
43 cm

212. Das Kind Lolottchen in einem zarten, hellkarierten Waschseidenkleidchen, mit weißem Kragen und Perlmutterknöpfchen. Gleiches Hütchen, weiße Schuhe RM 24.65 die Puppe ungekleidet RM 15.65

213 Das originelle Marienchen, im hellen Kleidchen mit rotem Dirndljäckchen, Zäckchen-Spitzenverzierungen, Kopftuch und weißen Schuhchen RM 22.15 die Puppe ungekleidet RM 15.65

Jupp mit der Schotten · Mütze und seine Schwester Ingeborg

214 im hellen Leinenhöschen und rostbrauner Joppe, dazu Seidenhemd mit Schnallenverschluß, flotter Schlips und Sportgürtel . . RM 26.65 Puppe ungekleidet RM 15.65

215 im rost · bunt · karierten Miederrock mit Goldknöpfchen verziert, ebenfalls mit Schottenkäppchen u. fliegenden Bändern und mit braunen Sandalen . . . . RM 24.65 als Hemdmatz . RM 15.65

216 Gisela. Es ist dieselbe Puppe wie Ingeborg, auch ebenso gekleidet, aber sie hat kurze blonde Locken aus Echthaar und kein Mützchen auf . . RM 38.— dieselbe als Hemdmatz RM 29.50

In the top row of the 1938-39 Kruse brochure are 11 examples of *Doll VIII, The German Child.* All had the same head.

PUPPE VIII
DAS DEUTSCHE KIND
52cm

207 **Für alle Puppen VIII passend,** ein hellseidenes Regenmäntelchen, mit braunem Sporthütchen und rotem Tupfschal, gleich hübsch für Jungens wie für Mädchen . . RM 8.50 abgebildet Florian Bild 203 mit dem Mantel und Hütchen dazu . . . . . RM 54.50

208 **Ein reizendes Nachtkleidchen** für die Mädelchen aus zartgemustertem Voile, mit weißen Pomponschuhchen . . . . . . RM 5.50 Abbildung: Ilsebill im Schlafanzug . . . . . RM 38.—

209 **Ein hellblauer Schlafanzug** für die Jungens, dunkelblau gepaspelt, mit weißen Schlafschuhchen . . . . RM 7.— Abbildung: Friedebald im Schlafanzug . . RM 42.50

210 **Ein Regencape** für die Mädchen aus hellbunt-kariertem Bembergseide, mit angearbeitetem Kapuzchen . . RM 5.— Abbildung: Susanne Bild 26 mit dem Cape . . RM 47.50

Noch etwas für die Mädchen:
211 **Ein gefüttertes Übergangsmäntelchen** aus hellrotem Wollstoff mit Rückenriegel und weißem Aufputz. Dazu das passende Hütchen . . RM 10.— Sehr reizend wäre Puppe „Jordi" in Weiß" mit dem Mantel RM 49.— oder, wie Abb., Ilsebill RM 51.

PUPPE I H
MIT ECHTEN HÄRCHEN
43cm

PUPPE XII H
DAS GLÜCKSKIND
45cm

218 **Ein Regencape für alle Puppen dieser Reihe passend,** aus heller, karierter Bembergseide, rot gefüttert, mit angesetztem Kapuzchen RM 5.— Abbildung: Brigittchen in Weiß RM 36.50 inkl. Cape . . . . RM 41.50

219 **Malte,** ein Kerlchen mit blondem Pagenkopf, hinten kurz geschoren, in einem blauweiß karierten Waschanzug mit weißem Krägelchen . . RM 39.— die Puppe ungekleidet RM 31.50

220 **Die Amrei.** Ihre blonden Locken hält ein Kopftuch. Sie trägt ein bunt-kariertes Röckchen und ein schwarzes Samtmieder mit Goldknöpfchen besetzt . . . . RM 33.— ungekleidet . . RM 26.50

221 **Ihr Bruder Hatti** trägt einen Sepplanzug, schwarze Höschen, kariertes Sporthemd mit Schnallenschluß und grüne, gestickte Hosenträger . . RM 34.50 als Hosenmatz . . RM 26.50

222 **Luischen vom Lande,** mit einem rotbunten Dirndlkleidchen, das mit schwarzem Samtband besetzt ist, dazu rotes Schürzchen und rote Schuhe . . . . RM 35.— als Hemdmatz . . RM 28.50

In the bottom row are examples of *Doll I* with painted hair and human-hair wigs.

Chart of Käthe Kruse Dolls

Number	Name	Date of Origin	Size	Head	Body	Other Information
Doll I	*Doll I*	1910	17 inches (43cm)	Made of cloth until about 1952, sewn on firmly, three pate seams, painted hair.	Nettle-cloth covering, arms sewn on, legs attached by two disc joints, wide hips, sewn-on thumbs until about 1930.	Eyes usually radiating irises.
Doll I, made by Kämmer & Reinhardt in 1911 only	*Doll I*	Early 1911	18 inches (45cm)	Swivel head, two hard halves, covered with fabric, hollow, one pate seam.	Nettle-cloth covering, jointed body, with and without ball-joints in knees.	Manufactured for a few months, very rare, so-called *flounder-body* with four or six joints.
Doll I H	*Doll I H*	From 1929 on (rare), mass-produced in 1936	First 17 inches (43cm), then 18 inches (45cm)	Sewn-on fabric head with wig; three pate seams. From about 1946 to about 1955, stamped-cardboard swivel head with fabric covering, one pate seam.	Like *Doll I*, with wide hips and sewn-on thumbs until about 1930.	Doll for 25th anniversary in 1936.
No number; variation of Doll I	*Bambino*	About 1923	About 10 inches (25cm)	Head of *Doll I*	Fabric body	Little doll with detachable wings from 1920s. See page 33.
No number; variation of Doll I	*Sternschnuppchen (Shooting Star)*	About 1932	14 inches (35cm)	Face half of *Doll I* sewn onto bonnet, painted hair.	Tricot covering, hands and feet not detailed. See page 33.	Initially there was a removable gold star on the head for Christmas.
Doll II	*Schlenkerchen (Dangles)*	1922	13 inches (33cm)	Sewn on loosely, one pate seam, painted hair.	Tricot covering, loosely attached arms and legs.	The only smiling Kruse doll, open-closed mouth.
Doll III	Unknown					
Doll IV	Unknown					
Doll Vs	*Träumerchen (Dreamer)* s=sleeping (Also called *Sandbaby*)	About 1925	18 inches-20 inches (45cm-50cm)	Fabric head, magnesite head beginning in 1935, painted hair, head weighted and unweighted, closed eyes.	Initially two models—A had tricot covering; B had stuffed body like the others. Foam with tricot covering beginning in 1965, arms and legs loosely attached, navel, later used small lead weights.	Size and weight of a newborn, 5-1/2 lbs. weighted, teaching doll weighted for infant care, unweighted as play doll. Called *Sandbaby* because body initially filled with sand.
Doll Vw	*Du Mein* w=awake	About 1925	18 inches-20 inches (45cm-50cm)	Like Vs above, but with open eyes.	Like Vs above, usually without navel.	Like *Träumerchen*, but with open eyes, weighted and unweighted, 3 to 5-1/2 lbs.
Doll Vw	*Du Mein*	Early 1930s	20 inches (50cm)	As above, but with human-hair wig, unweighted.	Nettle cloth or tricot, unweighted, without navel.	Face color usually heavily applied.
Doll VIs	*Träumerchen* s=sleeping (Also called *Sandbaby*)	About 1925	22 inches-24 inches (55cm-60cm)	Like Vs	Like Vs	Size and weight of 4-week-old baby, otherwise like Vs; weighted was 6 lbs.
Doll VIw	*Du Mein* w=awake	About 1925	22 inches-24 inches (55cm-60cm)	Like Vw	Like Vw	*Träumerchen* with open eyes as 4-week-old baby.
Doll VII	*The Small, Inexpensive Käthe Kruse Doll*	1927	14 inches (35cm)	Smaller Head I, sewn on firmly, three pate seams, cloth head, very rare with *Du Mein* head. See page 83.	Until about 1930 with broad hips and sewn-on arms, legs with disc joints.	Named *inexpensive* because of inflation, later discontinued.
Doll VIII	*The German Child* (Various names)	1929	21 inches (52cm)	Swivel-cloth head with wig, one pate seam, from 1946 until around 1955; also cardboard-swivel head with cloth cover, one pate seam; also plastic beginning in 1952.	Slender body with nettle-cloth cover, sewn-on arms, legs with disc joints.	One arm usually bent.

Number	Name	Date of Origin	Size	Head	Body	Other Information
Doll IX	*The Little German Child*	1929	14 inches (35cm)	Head like *Doll VIII*, swivel, initially with artificial hair, later human-hair wig, one pate seam, otherwise like *Doll VIII*.	Like *Doll VIII*	One arm usually bent.
Doll X	*The Little Käthe Kruse Doll*	About 1935	14 inches (35cm)	Originally swivel head of cloth, cardboard with painted hair beginning in 1946, one pate seam.	Slender cloth body, legs, with disc joints.	
Doll XI	Unknown					
Doll XII	*Hampelchen (Jumping Jack)*	Early 1930s	18 inches (45cm)	Head by Igor von Jakimow; also rarely Head I sewn on, painted hair, three pate seams.	Nettle-cloth cover, sewn-on arms, loosely sewn-on legs.	Could also stand with a button arrangement on back.
Doll XII	*Hampelchen*	Early 1930s	14 inches (35cm)	Sewn-on cloth head, three pate seams, painted hair.	As above	
Doll XII H	*Hampelchen*	Early 1930s	18 inches (45cm), later 19 inches (47cm)	As above, but with wig, three pate seams.	Sewn-on arms, loosely attached legs.	Could also stand with a button arrangement on back.
Doll XII H	*Hampelchen (Also called Child of Fortune)*	Early 1930s	18 inches (45cm), later 19 inches (47cm)	Sewn on firmly with wig, three pate seams.	Sewn-on arms, loosely attached legs.	Body, hands and feet more simply modeled, thus somewhat cheaper.
Doll XII B	*The Little Baby Hampelschatz*	End of 1940s	16 inches (40cm)	Head I sewn on, painted hair or wig.	Sewn-on arms, loosely attached legs.	
Doll XII/I	*Hampelchen*	End of 1940s	18 inches (45cm)	Sewn-on head with wig.	Slender body with disc joints like *Doll I*.	
No number	*The Slim Grandchild*	1952	19 inches (47cm)	Swivel plastic head with straight and sideways glance, human-hair wig, heart-shaped mouth.	Very thin cloth body, sewn-on arms, legs with disc joints.	Doll for 40th anniversary. Made only short time; thin legs were difficult to stuff.
No number	*Käthe Kruse Celluloid Doll*	About 1955-58		Celluloid with human-hair wig.	Celluloid, also cloth body.	Produced by the firm of Schildkröt.

This chart was compiled from data on several original brochures and from other research. In several instances, precise dates couldn't be determined. To confuse things more, the Kruse workshops frequently filled special orders. The Kruses also improvised. Käthe Kruse tried many ideas, and exceptions were common. The chart includes *Dolls I-XII.* In several cases, there are variations of a doll. Only five different doll heads are known. These are *Dolls I, II, V/VI, VIII* and *XII. Doll XII* had the von Jakimow head. *Dolls III, IV* and *XI* have never been found. No old Kruse brochures list them. They are not mentioned in books written by Käthe Kruse and are unknown to the Kruse workshops, family members and experts. It is possible these numbers were for dolls that were planned but never manufactured. Dolls with painted hair could be ordered with human-hair wigs beginning in 1929. The 21-inch (52cm) *German Child* generally had Head VIII. In rare cases, Head VIII was also used on the 18-inch (45cm) doll. Porcelain-head dolls use the term *kurbelkopf,* meaning *turning head.* The Kruse brochure here uses the word *drehkopf,* meaning *turning neck.*

Doll I

Kämmer & Reinhardt produced *Doll I* from the beginning of 1911 until that summer. They manufactured the dolls using Käthe Kruse patterns. Käthe Kruse canceled the contract because she thought their dolls didn't meet her standards. See page 22 for more information.

Doll I was produced for only a few months by Kämmer & Reinhardt. It is a coveted collector's item because it is so rare.

It was 18 inches (45 cm) tall and had a swivel head like the ones on porcelain dolls. The head had a firm facemask. The firm pate was hollow, covered with fabric and had a vertical pate seam and crossing seam on the head. These are the only Kruse dolls with ball-joints in the knees. See page 102 for more information. Arms and hips were jointed.

Käthe Kruse began producing *Doll I* in the fall of 1911. It was 17 inches (43 cm) tall and had a sewn-on, firmly attached cloth head. The eyes usually had a painted, radiating iris. Arms were sewn on, legs had disc joints and hips were wide and well-developed. The thumbs were sewn onto the hands. All body parts looked remarkably natural. They were stuffed with water-repellent materials, such as reindeer or deer hair.

The expressive and lively faces made the early dolls impressive. There is an unusual fascination radiating from them. One of these dolls is the *Peasant Lad Fritz*, pictured on pages 68 and 69.

There are several seams on his head. The face was sewn to the back of the head and the neck with a circular seam. This seam goes over the top of the head from one ear to the other. Three seams went from the middle of the head over the pate. Two seams run from the corners of the mouth to the chin. The head was sewn onto the body.

Doll I had a chubby child's body with wide hips. Beginning at the neck, two seams went down the back, two seams ran along the front of the body and two seams were on each side. The arms were sewn on and had seams the entire length of both sides.

Palms were attached to the wrists. The thumbs were sewn on separately, and the fingers were individually seamed. The hip joints were reinforced with cardboard discs called *disc joints*. A cotter pin was used to fasten the legs to the body.

The legs were lavishly worked. Käthe Kruse considered five pieces of cloth with five seams necessary for the legs to look natural. The knees were sculpted with filler material. The foot was sewn on in front, and the sole was strengthened with a cardboard disc. The toes were individually seamed. See page 42 for more information.

This doll was the only one produced from 1911-1922.

The doll was dressed as a boy and a girl and received different names depending on its costume. In this way, different dolls could be distinguished in the catalog.

For example, *Doll I* in a blue coachman's coat with white pants, a piqued cap and straw shoes was called *Michel*. He is shown on page 15. *Red Riding Hood* was dressed in a red and white checked skirt with a hand-knit jacket and cap, red socks and shoes of raffia. She is pictured on pages 7 and 15. *Jockerle* was dressed in green overalls, a long-sleeved shirt, hand-knit wool cap and gray-green long stockings. *Margaretchen* wore a peasant dress, hand-knit wool jacket and cap. Both are pictured on page 14.

The four dolls were offered in the 1952 brochure as the well-known "original Käthe Kruse *Doll I*."

Early *Doll I*, left, produced around 1916 by Käthe Kruse workshops. *Doll I,* right, manufactured by Kämmer &
Reinhardt. This one is almost 1 inch (2cm) taller.

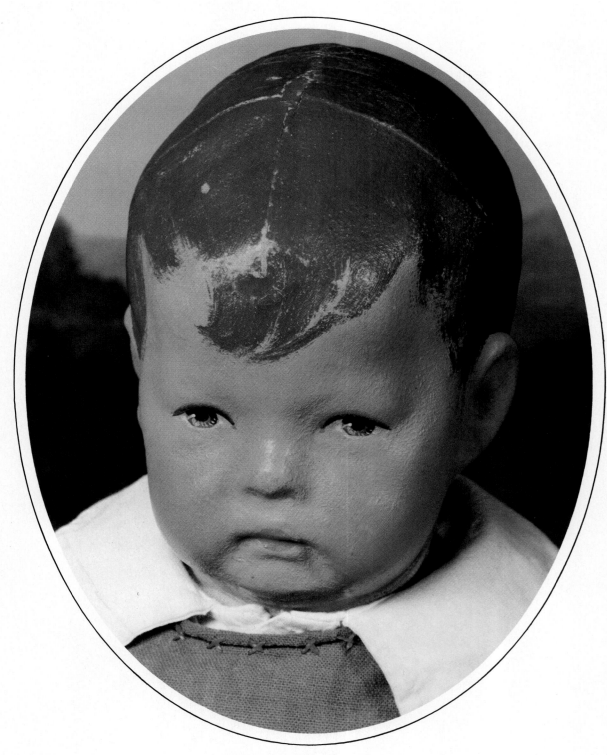

Doll I as Peasant Lad Fritz.

Doll I, from 1913, 17 inches (43cm) tall, sewn-on cloth head, sewn-on thumbs, wide hips and eyes with radiating irises. Original clothing for *Peasant Lad Fritz.*

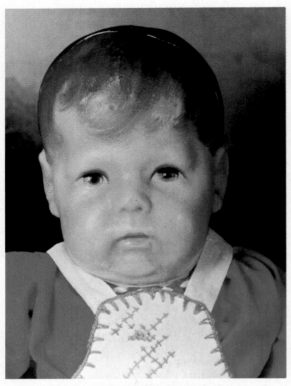

Doll I, around 1915, 17 inches (43cm), sewn-on cloth head, sewn-on thumbs, wide hips and eyes with radiating irises.

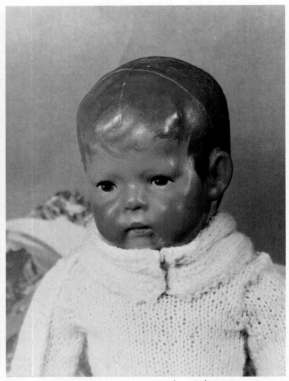

Doll I, around 1918, 17 inches (43cm), sewn-on cloth head, sewn-on thumbs, wide hips and eyes with radiating irises. Cheeks, ears and mouth were painted red.

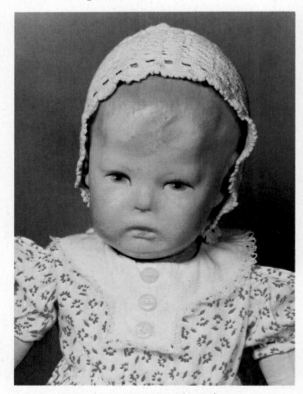

Doll I, around 1920, 17 inches (43cm), sewn-on cloth head, sewn-on thumbs, wide hips and eyes with radiating irises.

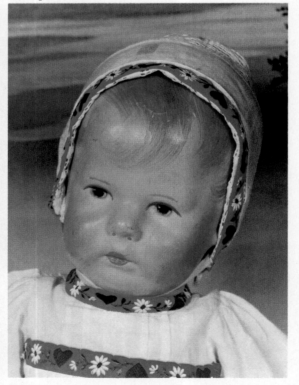

Doll I, around 1930, 17 inches (43cm), sewn-on cloth head and thumbs. Hips were no longer as wide.

Sternschnuppchen

This *Doll I* version was first made around 1932. A cloth bonnet was stitched directly onto the face mask of this doll. The head and the loose arms and legs were stuffed softly as was the small tricot-covered, baby-like body. Fingers and toes were not seamed as they were in *Doll I*. See photo on page 33.

Sternschnuppchen, 14 inches (35cm). Original clothing and bonnet. For Christmas, this doll had a gold paper star on its head. Its name means *shooting star*.

Doll I H

Doll I was made with a human-hair wig in 1936 in honor of the firm's 25th anniversary. Except in rare instances, hair had been painted before 1936.

Doll first available with firmly attached cloth head and three pate seams. It was also manufactured with cardboard swivel head from around 1946-1955. The head was hollow, covered on the outside with cloth, and had one pate seam.

Top left: Around 1928, 17 inches (43cm), radiating irises, sewn-on thumbs, wide hips. A very early doll. Top right: Around 1935, 18 inches (45cm). Bottom left: Around 1940, 18 inches (45cm). Bottom right: Around 1950, 18 inches (45cm), restored.

Doll I H, around 1936, 18 inches (45cm), sewn-on cloth head and radiating irises. This doll is especially well-preserved.

Doll II, Schlenkerchen

Doll I conquered the world's hearts for 11 years. *Schlenkerchen* arrived in 1922 as a Käthe Kruse innovation. It was 13 inches (33cm) tall and dressed as a boy or girl. It was given names like *Maxl, Ulla, Adi, Mädi, Lucy* and *Troll.*

The doll had an open-closed mouth and a smiling face. The cloth head had one pate seam. The small, chubby body used a wire skeleton for flexibility and was covered with tricot. *Schlenkerchen* had loosely attached head, arms and legs and is often confused with *Hampelchen, Doll XII* for that reason. *Doll II* was manufactured for a short time. It was not offered in the 1938-39 catalog, and it is very rare today. The soft body was more fragile than other dolls because of the wire skeleton. More information about the manufacture of this popular Käthe Kruse doll is found on page 48.

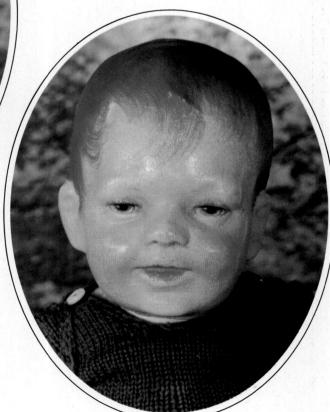

Schlenkerchen, the only Kruse doll having open eyes with painted eyelashes, smiling face and open-closed mouth.

Schlenkerchen, sitting, around 1925, 13 inches (33cm), open-closed mouth, smiling face, loosely sewn-on cloth head, loosely attached arms and legs. The standing *Doll VIII, The German Child*, 1930, is rare.

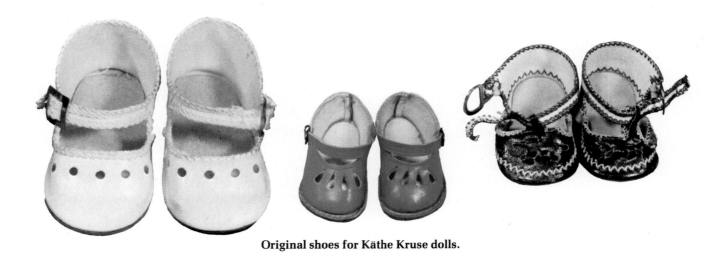

Original shoes for Käthe Kruse dolls.

Doll V/VI, Träumerchen/Du Mein

Three *Träumerchen*, weighted, and one *Du Mein*, weighing 2 lbs., from 1950s. All have magnesite heads, wrapped bodies with tricot covers. Sizes from left, 20 inches (50cm), 19 inches (47cm), 20 inches (50cm) and 24 inches (60cm).

Träumerchen came out around 1925 as a doll to teach baby care. It had closed eyes. Soon it became a highly coveted play doll. The same doll, with open eyes, came out a short time later and was called *Du Mein*.

Both dolls were 20 inches (50cm) tall and weighed 5-1/2 pounds. They were made to resemble a newborn. They had cloth heads and were weighted with little bags of sand distributed in the body. The nickname *Sandbaby* comes from that. Later, lead weights were used. These dolls had the weight of a real baby and would lie in the holder's arms like one.

The head was heavy and loose. It rolled back and forth without stopping and had to be supported. A navel was sewn onto the little abdomen of *Träumerchen*.

Both dolls were available for children to play with without weights and were manufactured in two models. Model A had a colored tricot covering that could be cleaned or taken off and washed. Model B had a nettle-cloth body and was stuffed with deer hair like other Kruse dolls. This model was simpler and cheaper.

Model A was later produced with a new technique. Contours were sculpted of cotton batting over a movable skeleton. The skeleton extended down into the fingertips, and the body was covered with tricot. The joints were extremely flexible and invisible.

The same *Du Mein* doll was offered with a wig in the 1930s. This wig was a masterpiece. It was made of finely tied human hair so thin the scalp shone through like a real baby. This *Du Mein* was lighter, was not sand-filled and had no navel.

Träumerchen and *Du Mein* were available in sizes 18 inches to 24 inches (45cm to 60cm). The most collectable are the early models with cloth heads. Collectors also enjoy the dolls equipped with magnesite heads, which were produced beginning in 1935. Collectors have little interest in the plastic heads manufactured since 1965.

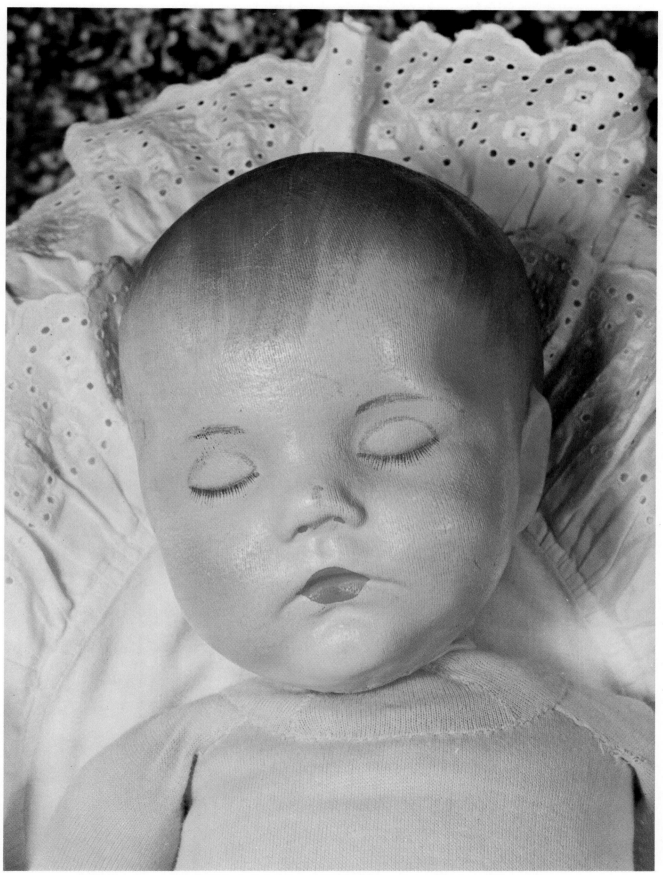

Träumerchen, around 1928, cloth head, weighted with navel, excellent condition, very rare.

Du Mein, end of the 1920s, 20 inches (50cm), unweighted, cloth head, radiating irises.

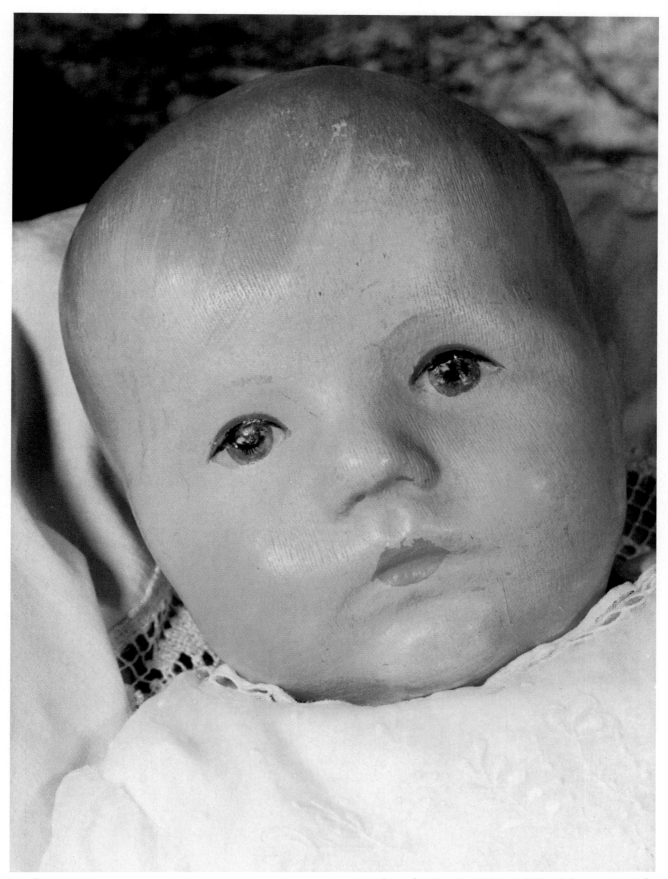

This *Du Mein* with sewn-on cloth head is very rare. It is 20 inches (50cm) tall and weighs 5-1/2 lbs. It has a wrapped body with a tricot cover and a sewn-on navel.

Left: *Du Mein,* around 1937, 20 inches (50cm), magnesite head. **Right:** First *Little Kruse Doll VII* of 1927 with sewn-on little *Du Mein* cloth head, sewn-on thumbs, wide hips. It is very rare.

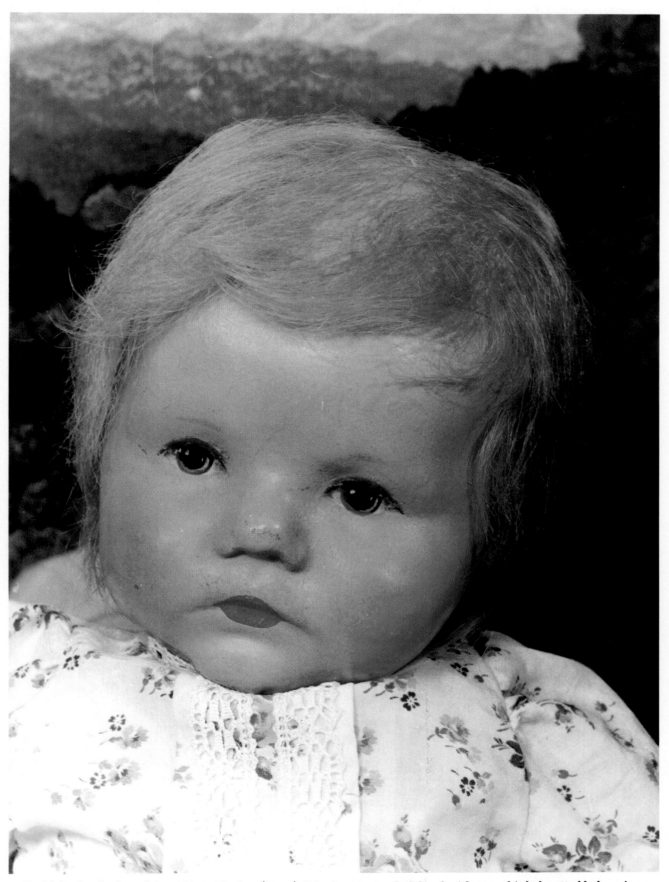

Du Mein, beginning of the 1930s, 20 inches (50cm). It had sewn-on cloth head with rare, thinly knotted baby wig so scalp shimmered through. It had radiating irises, unweighted, wrapped body with tricot cover.

Doll VII,
The Small, Inexpensive Käthe Kruse Doll

Not many people could afford *Doll I* during the inflation of the 1920s. Käthe Kruse's smaller *Doll I* came out in 1927. It was 14 inches (35cm) tall. Its name was a reminder that it was less expensive than the other dolls. The word *inexpensive* was dropped after a few years.

This doll was also called *Inflation Doll* in doll circles. This was not intended to indicate a lesser quality. *Doll VII* is no new doll type, but a version of *Doll I.*

It had a firmly sewn-on cloth head with painted hair and three pate seams. Until about 1930, it had sewn-on thumbs and wide hips. The arms were sewn on, and the legs had disc joints. The body was made more delicate in 1930. *Doll VII* was offered from 23.50 to 29 marks in the 1927 catalog. The price differed depending on the clothing.

Doll VII was also available with human hair. A photograph is shown below. This version never received a different name. The first Käthe Kruse dolls came out with human-hair wigs in 1929. Dolls with painted hair could also be ordered with human-hair wigs.

Doll VII was equipped with Head I and sometimes with the smaller Head V of *Du Mein*. This surprises many collectors.

The Small Käthe Kruse Doll, Head I, around 1930, 14 inches (35cm), sewn-on cloth head, rare human-hair wig, sewn-on thumbs, wide hips.

Top left: *The Little Käthe Kruse Doll*, around 1927, 14 inches (35cm), sewn-on cloth head of *Doll Vw*, sewn-on thumbs, wide hips.

Lower left, *The Little Käthe Kruse Doll*, head of *Doll Vw*, around 1929, 14 inches (35cm), sewn-on cloth head, sewn-on thumbs, wide hips.

Above: *The Little Käthe Kruse Doll*, Head I, around 1930, 14 inches (35cm), sewn-on cloth head, sewn-on thumbs, wide hips.

Doll VIII, The German Child

The Kruse doll production was enriched in 1929 with *Doll VIII, The German Child*. It was larger than her other dolls and was 21 inches (52cm) tall. It was the first Käthe Kruse doll made with a swivel head and human-hair wig.

It is the only play doll modeled after one of Käthe Kruse's children. Friedebald, 8, was sculpted by Igor von Jakimow. The forms for *Doll VIII* were patterned after this bust. This boy doll received the name *Friedebald*.

Friedebald became *Ilsebill* by fitting the same head with a girl's wig. This pair soon became a great hit of the Käthe Kruse collection. Children could style the hair of their dolls. *Friedebald* soon had many sisters who shared his head. They included *Susanne, Flora, Jordi, Leila, Renate, Annemarie, Veronika* and *Leonore*. Some examples are shown on pages 62 and 63.

Doll VIII was first manufactured with a cloth head and one pate seam. A cardboard swivel head with a cloth covering and one pate seam were used from 1946-1955. It was also manufactured with a plastic head beginning in 1952. The legs had disc joints.

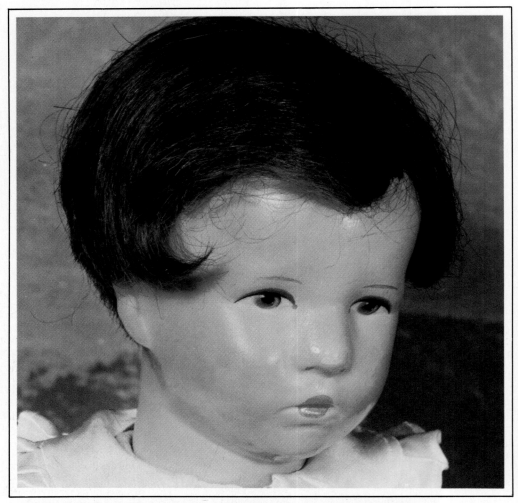

Käthe Kruse preferred blond and brown wigs. Black ones were rare. All wigs were made with long hair. On boys, the hair was cut.

Ilsebill around 1930. *Friedebald* around 1940. Both dolls 21 inches (52cm), cloth-swivel heads. Original boy and girl wigs.

Ilsebill in the Wind. Brochure photo by Jochen Kruse.

Doll VIII, early 1930s, 21 inches (52cm), cloth-swivel head, radiating irises.

Doll IX, The Little German Child

Doll VII, the small version of *Doll I,* sold extremely well. As a result Käthe Kruse decided to include a small version of *Doll VIII. The Little German Child* was 14 inches (35cm) tall. It had a cloth head and was made like its big brother.

Doll IX was also dressed as a boy and a girl. The number of variations increased each year by changing wigs, clothing and name but keeping the same head. This was perhaps a unique production philosophy. *Doll IX* names included *Rapunzel, Finusch, Bertchen, Roderich, Alice* and *Macke.*

Doll VIII, The German Child, was sold in the 1929-30 catalog from 37.50 to 46 marks. *Doll IX, The Little German Child,* was priced from 25 to 32 marks. The price depended on the doll's clothing.

Roderich, with cloth-swivel head, 14 inches (35cm) tall. New original clothing with leather school bag. Doll is shown above in the box with wrapping. The tag says *Made in U.S. Zone, Germany,* which indicates about 1948. A doll in this condition, with this clothing, is a rare collector's item.

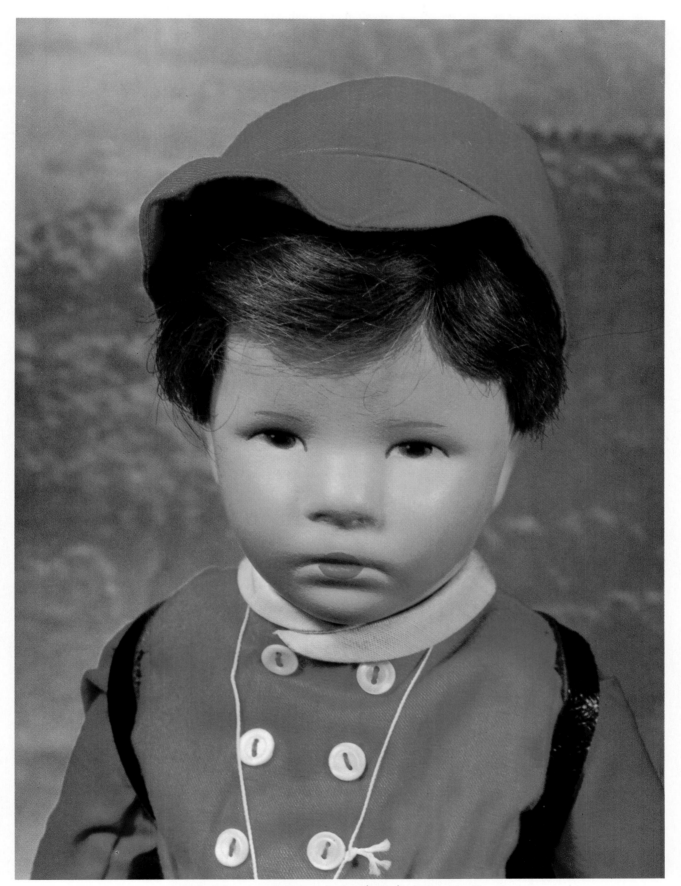

Roderich, around 1948, 14 inches (35cm), cloth-swivel head.

Doll IX, The Little German Child, early 1930s, 14 inches (35cm), cloth-swivel head, original boy's wig.

Doll X, The Little Käthe Kruse Doll

This doll, brought out in 1935, was not a new doll type. It was identical to *Doll VII* except it had a swivel head instead of a firmly attached one. It also had painted hair. It was listed at 13.75 marks with a shirt and 19.75 marks fully clothed in the 1937-38 price list.

The Little Käthe Kruse Doll in a streetcar conductor's uniform, around 1935, 14 inches (35cm), cloth-swivel head. Cap and smock are original.

The Little Käthe Kruse Doll, 1948, 14 inches (35cm), cloth-swivel head. Tag says *Made in U.S. Zone, Germany.*

Doll XII, Hampelchen

Hampelchen caused quite a stir when it debuted in 1931. It had no movable disc joints in the legs. See page 103 for an example. The arms and legs were sewn on loosely. This was designed to encourage children to play with it. The doll could stand by using a button on its back that could be attached with a band to the thighs. An example of this variation is shown on page 109.

The head was sculpted by Igor von Jakimow, an artist related to the family. This doll sometimes had the head of *Doll I*. In both cases, it was a firmly attached cloth head with painted hair and three pate seams. *Hampelchen* was manufactured in sizes of 14 inches (35cm), 16 inches (40cm) and 18 inches (45cm). Information on *Hampelchen* versions *XII B* and *XII/I* is listed on page 65.

Hampelchen, early 1930s, 18 inches (45cm), sewn-on cloth head of *Doll I*, Bavarian costume. Like Gulliver, *Hampelchen* strides over houses and roofs.

Original shoes for Käthe Kruse doll.

Hampelchen, 1943, 18 inches (45cm), sewn-on cloth head modeled by Igor von Jakimow.

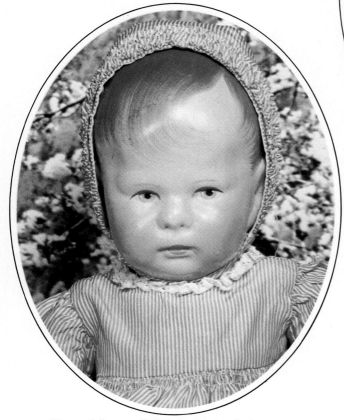

Hampelchen, 1940s, 14 inches (35cm), sewn-on cloth head of *Doll I.*

Hampelchen, called *Baby Hampelschatz,* around 1950, 16 inches (40cm), sewn-on cloth head of *Doll I.*

Doll XII H, The Child of Fortune

When a human-hair wig was added to *Hampelchen* with the charming Jakimow head, it received the extra letter H. It appeared in the early 1930s. This *Hampelchen* was called *The Child of Fortune* and was 18 inches (45cm) tall. "The legs and hands were developed somewhat less finely," the firm's brochure said. It was less expensive as a result. For example, in 1937 the doll cost between 26.50 and 34.50 marks.

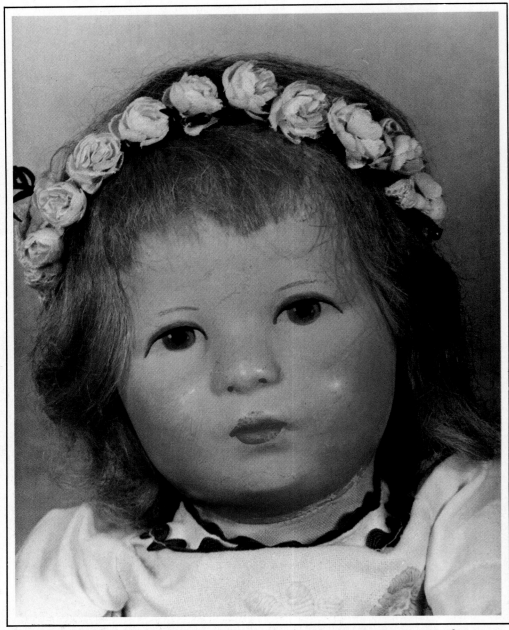

This beautiful doll has a little damage because of use, but no cracks. See page 104 for more information. *Hampelchen* had a radiating iris on rare occasions. See page 108 for more information. *Hampelchen* was offered as a boy or a girl and used the same head with different wigs. It was given the names *Micke, Gert* and *Lilo* in the 1937-38 catalog. In 1939 it was named *Amrei, Matti* and *Luischen*.

Hampelchen, nicknamed *Child of Fortune* because it cost less to manufacture, 18 inches (45cm), sewn-on cloth head by Igor von Jakimow.

Doll XII H, Hampelchen, also called ***Child of Fortune,*** around 1940, 18 inches (45cm), sewn-on cloth head by Igor von Jakimow.

The Slim Grandchild

The Slim Grandchild introduced the modern era for Käthe Kruse dolls. It premiered in 1952 for the firm's 40th anniversary. This doll was 19 inches (47cm) tall with a plastic head. It had a straight or sideways glance and a thin body.

Its slimness was its downfall. The thin arms and legs were difficult to stuff. This doll was produced only for a short time. It had a human-hair wig, and the face was painted by hand. It had a heart-shaped mouth. In other respects, it was a typical Käthe Kruse doll.

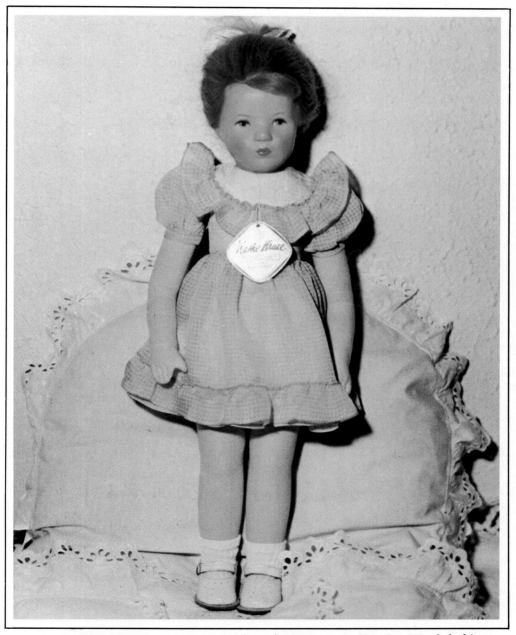

The Slim Grandchild, 1952, 19 inches (47cm), plastic-swivel head, original clothing, heart-shaped mouth.

Käthe Kruse Celluloid Dolls

Käthe Kruse remained faithful for more than 40 years to her basic principle of soft, cloth dolls. She had to make compromises in the 1950s because the firm had financial problems. She needed to make less-expensive dolls. She agreed to work with the Celluloid factory Schildkröt. The first Kruse/Schildkröt dolls were shown at the sixth German Toy Fair in Nuremberg. They were made of Celluloid or Tortulon, a mixture of Celluloid and plastic.

But Käthe Kruse didn't give Schildkröt the original head forms of her dolls. She gave permission instead to copy the heads of *Dolls VIII* and *XII* for a fee. These heads had human-hair wigs or, sometimes, sculpted hair. They were attached to cloth or Celluloid bodies.

At first the eyes were painted. Later, glass or plastic eyes were set in. For the most part, these dolls were not successful and after 2 or 3 years were no longer produced. From 1958-1977, Schildkröt owned 70% of the Käthe Kruse Play Dolls Limited.

Marking of the Käthe Kruse Celluloid dolls manufactured by Schildkröt. It bore Schildkröt trademark and Käthe Kruse signature.

Left: Around 1958, 18 inches (45cm), Celluloid swivel head with original wig, Celluloid body. Right: Around 1958, Celluloid swivel head, original wig, cloth body.

Käthe Kruse Dolls with Plastic Heads

Käthe Kruse dolls were made with plastic heads beginning about 1955. Cloth heads became too expensive to produce. Painting on plastic faces looks nice, but one tends to look back at the early cloth heads with a certain nostalgia.

Eyes and mouth were colored with a pattern. The pupils and other details were painted by hand. The expensive human-hair wigs are still used today. Most of the bodies have been plastic for many years.

The beautiful, carefully worked clothing is still remarkable. Combining clothes with various wigs makes it possible to offer about 80 dolls today. There are only four head types. Modern manufacturing finally made its connection with earlier traditions.

The doll pictured on the title page of the 1981-82 catalog, shown below, still radiates a special quality. The dolls are presented in beautiful color photographs consistent with their image. The Käthe Kruse high-quality standards are still maintained.

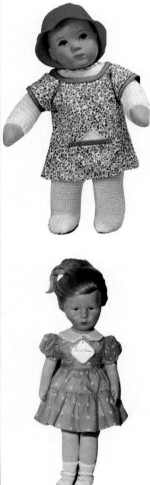

Title page of the 1981-82 brochure. The dolls on top left and right were taken from this catalog.

Original Doll I Body Pattern

The envelope from Nov. 7, 1911, is in Käthe Kruse's handwriting. It says, "The final body pattern sent to Ilmenau. We will now use this. Waist size 10 inches (26cm), hips 14 inches (34cm), height 13 inches (33cm)." This is the original body pattern designed by Käthe Kruse for the world-famous *Doll I.* The height of 13 inches (33cm) refers to shoulder height. A few pieces of this detailed body pattern are published here for the first time.

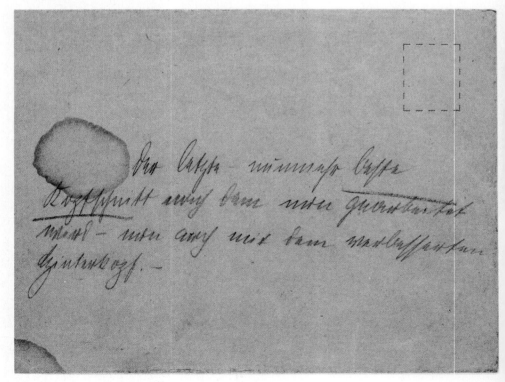

Original Doll I Head Pattern

This envelope contains the head pattern of *Doll I* designed by Käthe Kruse. It was a trade secret guarded for many decades. Her handwritten note says, "The last, and to be sure best, head pattern from which we will now work. This also has the improved back of the head." As described earlier, the head was covered with cloth and had three pate seams. On the opposite page are a few pieces of this pattern. The head was softly stuffed, painted with oil paints and sewn firmly onto the body.

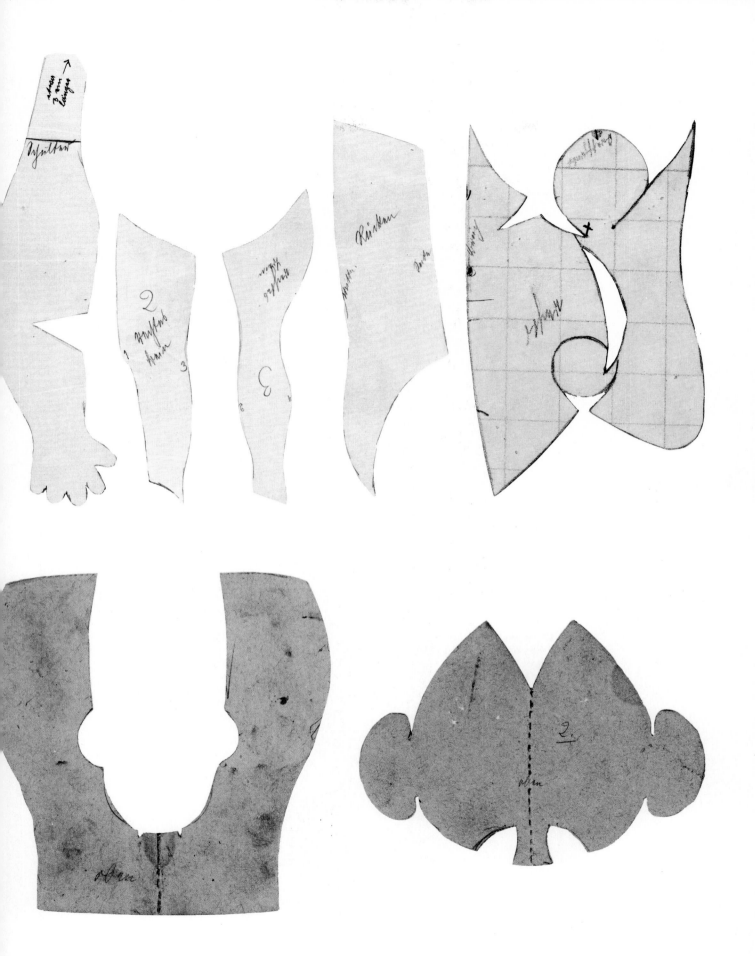

Bodies

Body types and production are described on pages 46 to 48. There we discussed whether the body had sewn-on legs or disc joints, whether the head was firmly attached to the body or whether there was a swivel head, and whether it had sewn-on thumbs or wide hips. For *Doll I*, described on page 66, there is even a description of the number and direction of most body seams.

On pages 100 and 101, details about the original head and body pattern of *Doll I* are shown.

Many collectors can still benefit from pictures of the various body types. The dolls are shown in scale so the various sizes can be compared.

A typical Celluloid is shown on page 98. The various positions pictured on page 47 show how *Hampelchen's* flexible legs could be positioned.

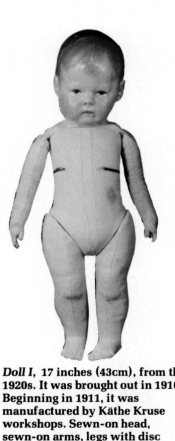

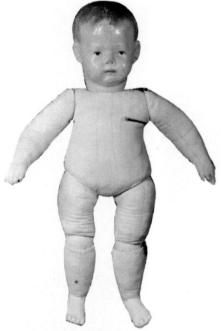

Doll I, 17 inches (43cm), from the 1920s. It was brought out in 1910. Beginning in 1911, it was manufactured by Käthe Kruse workshops. Sewn-on head, sewn-on arms, legs with disc joints, thumbs sewn on individually, wide hips. Many cloth pieces were used to form the body.

Doll I, 18 inches (45cm), beginning of 1911, probably manufactured by Kämmer & Reinhardt, with swivel head, joints in the arms and legs, rare ball-joints in the knees. The body is not as well-stuffed, nor as well-shaped. "Flounder-like body," as Käthe Kruse called it. This doll is very rare.

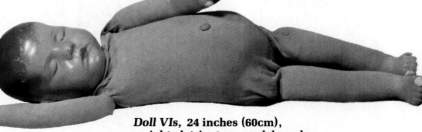

Doll VIs, 24 inches (60cm), weighted, tricot covered, loosely attached arms and indented legs, sewn-on navel.

Doll I H, 17 inches (43cm), beginning in 1928. Body like *Doll I* with wide hips, legs with disc joints.

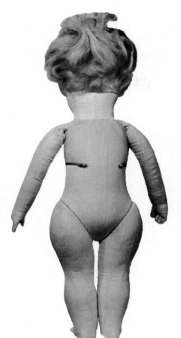

Doll I H, rear view with visible head seam.

Doll I H, 18 inches (45cm), slim hips and legs, legs with disc joints. Beginning in 1936.

Doll II, 13 inches (33cm), tricot, loosely attached arms and legs.

Doll VII, 14 inches (35cm), reduced body of *Doll I,* wide hips, legs with disc joints.

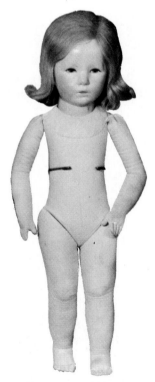

Doll VIII, 21 inches (52cm), large thin body, legs with disc joints, swivel head.

Doll IX, 14 inches (35cm), reduced body of *Doll VIII,* legs with disc joints, swivel head.

Doll XII, 18 inches (45cm), loosely attached arms and indented legs, sewn-on head.

Restore a Doll?

Placing a Käthe Kruse doll in a glass case with a broken nose, scratched or cracked face and in a dirty or ragged condition is a matter of taste. This condition is tolerated by many collectors because they love their dolls and are pleased with the way they look. But sometimes expert care is necessary to save a rare doll.

Käthe Kruse dolls are not fragile, but they can still be damaged. The colors can be worn, for example, if a child washes its doll, then puts it in the sun or too near a heater to dry. This applies even to oil paint. A cracked spot on the face is worse than if the red cheeks of a doll have been rubbed or kissed off, or if the color has faded. If paint has been cracked, air gets into hollow spaces and raises the paint layer. It is only a matter of time before the paint begins to flake and the cloth covering peeks through.

Superficial restoration will not save the doll. This wouldn't reach the hollow spaces beneath the crack. Dolls with cracks on their faces or heads must be taken to a restorer. There they will be expertly patched using heat and a special beeswax. This fills and firms the hollow spaces so the paint can't flake.

This is a type of welding technique. It is the same restoration procedure used for oil paintings on canvas. The layman can't do this properly. The outside of the doll doesn't change, and the cracks will still be visible as lines. But the doll is saved from further decay.

Children weren't as careful playing with Käthe Kruse dolls as they were with porcelain-head dolls. The nose is damaged or worn on almost a third of Käthe Kruse dolls that have been played with. A good restorer can redo the nose so the appearance won't be changed. But there are risks involved in such a process.

Modeling clay can be used by amateurs to sculpt the point of the nose. Washable watercolors can then reproduce the color. With any luck the original beauty will be replaced. If not, simply remove the modeling clay.

Older dolls with worn facial color due to hard play are sometimes painted. This can cause the doll to lose its original characteristics. I would recommend the paint be removed by a restorer and the doll be properly painted.

Cracking or other damage left untreated causes layers of paint to flake.

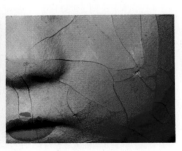

Example of cracking in face of a Kruse doll painted recently. The painting is not like the original.

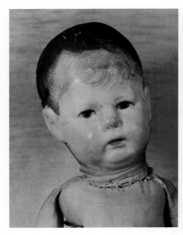

Before
Large areas of color are lacking on the forehead and head. Damage to the nose and cheeks is as disturbing as the amateur painting of the mouth.

Before
This *Doll I H* has been to a doll doctor once. It was not painted like the original, especially in the choice of color. The eyebrows and fire-red, heart-shaped mouth are also incorrect.

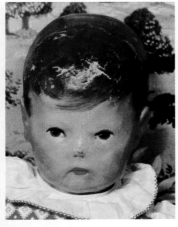

Before
Hair, eyes, cheeks and mouth were painted on later with strong color. Especially disturbing is the atypical painted hair wave.

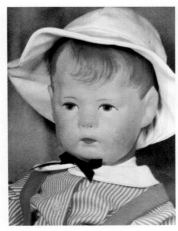

After
Missing layers of color were applied with a palette knife. The end of the nose was finished. Hair and face were partially painted. The mouth was completely painted. This type of work costs $60 to $100.

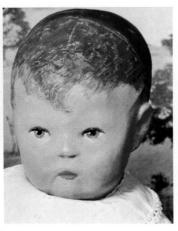

After
This *Doll I* was repainted after restoring the nose and head. Whether this doll has regained its typical Kruse face is a matter of judgment.

After
This doll was made a "genuine" *Doll I H* after removing the paint and reapplying new colors. The doll on the left had cracks in her face welded.

Clothing

Käthe Kruse dolls wore colorful costumes. The dolls were made practically so the clothes could be taken off and put on. Käthe Kruse designed the clothes at first, but later Anne Kurreck was given this task. Examples of her work are shown on page 23.

Almost all early clothing was manufactured by cottage labor. The dolls were dressed at first like the porcelain-head dolls of 1910. But Käthe Kruse very quickly developed her own unmistakable style. At first glance, it appears porcelain-head dolls were dressed more luxuriously and expensively. But on closer inspection, the work often leaves much to be desired. The material was often a lower quality.

Käthe Kruse clothing was the opposite. Close inspection shows clothing that appears simple was actually carefully worked. The materials were of high quality, and suits and dresses were usually lined. Cottons were preferred. Red-on-red patterns were the favorite colors. Prints are not always as small as you would think it should be for dolls. Large checks and big flowers were used. Large hats were used in various forms. For example, cloches, berets, sun and straw hats showed only the little face.

Everything was manufactured with hooks and eyes or buttons to easily dress and undress the dolls. Nothing tore easily so the clothing could be pulled. Jackets, pants, caps, scarves and shoes were knitted by hand. Dresses and skirts were embroidered and had smocking and ruffles.

Lace was used sparingly. Usually only narrow pieces were used as insets or for a little collar. Shoes and socks were always precisely matched to the clothing. Simple or country costumes often used woven or crocheted straw or bast shoes. The underwear was also sewn very carefully. Page 107 shows some examples.

Käthe Kruse didn't always dress her dolls simply and practically. She knew children wanted to admire their darlings in their Sunday best or in festival costumes. Elegant doll clothing was manufactured in 1928-39 for *Doll VIII*. It was made of expensive materials like velvet, silk, organdy, chiffon and batiste. The girl dolls also had elaborate curled wigs decorated with bows, wreaths and flowers.

Käthe Kruse also liked beautiful native costumes. When the small Kruse doll first appeared in the catalog in 1927, two favorite native costume couples were offered. These were a Dutch couple and a Biedermeier couple. Other native-costumed couples followed, primarily in Bavarian and Salzburg costumes. There were also wool, felt and imitation-fur coats, sports clothes and ski suits.

Keep the original clothing at any price and leave it on the doll. If a ragged doll without its original clothing is discovered, the collector faces a challenge. Clothe the doll as closely as possible to the original. Find old material to make clothes. Or look for old doll clothes.

It was fun to have original clothing copied for the four most famous dolls from the first catalog. These were *Michel*, *Red Riding Hood*, *Jockerle* and *Margaretchen*. They are pictured on pages 14 and 15. The dolls were still offered in these costumes in the 1952 catalog.

Top and middle rows: Dolls in original clothing. *Farmer Boy Fritz, Dolls I, VIII, IX and XII.* **Bottom row:** Recent clothing modeled from the original. All heads are of *Doll VIII.*

Characteristics and Markings

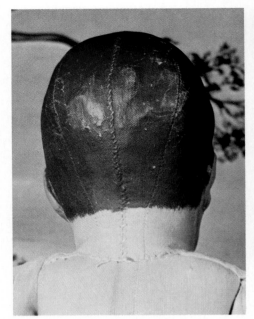

Doll I and all cloth-head dolls with firmly attached heads have three pate seams.

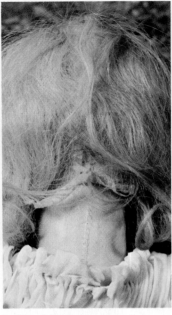

Dolls with cloth-covered swivel heads have one pate seam.

Wide- and narrow-hipped dolls. Wide hips were made until about 1930.

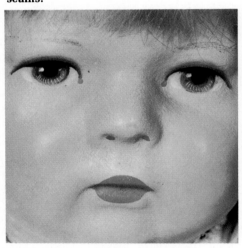

Early *Dolls I and I H,* had radiating irises.

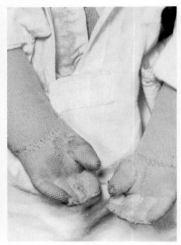

In earlier dolls, the thumb is sewn on individually.

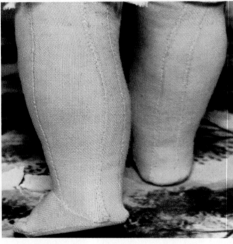

Early dolls had five leg seams so they would look real.

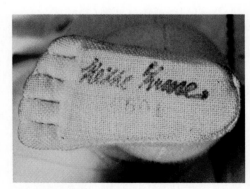

Original Käthe Kruse signature from left sole is shown above.

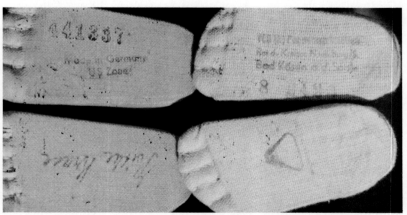

Sole on top left is stamp of the U.S. Zone. On the right is stamp *VEB* with triangle. Both soles were stamped during the U.S. occupation in Donauwörth, as well as with the VEB works in Bad Kösen.

Hampelchen with loosely attached arms and legs. It could stand using the button and band on its back.

Sternschnuppchen with face half of *Doll I* and firmly sewn-on bonnet. In original clothing.

Doll VIII as Christmas angel. Not original clothing.

Träumerchen from the 1930s in a motion study. It had a magnesite head.

The loosely attached head permitted positions resembling a baby.

Conceived as a doll for infant care, *Träumerchen* soon became a popular play doll.

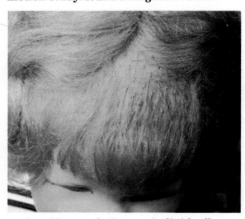

Locks of human hair were individually attached by hand to the wigs.

Two labels attached around the wrist or the neck of Käthe Kruse dolls. Back of the label also carried the message, *U.S. Zone Germany,* after 1945, during American occupation. Name of the individual doll was often noted in handwriting on this tag. At right, the trademark.

Predecessors, Copies and Prices

Forerunners of Käthe Kruse Dolls

Cloth or rag dolls have been made for centuries. Commercial manufacture of rag dolls began in 1851. Augusta Montanari introduced this doll in London. These rag dolls developed into the Dawdler dolls, the Peddler and Fortune-Teller Dolls in England.

Georg Hetzel caused quite a stir in Germany in 1865 with his dolls with wax face halves covered with cloth. Then the head was stuffed. Fritz Bierschenk further developed the cloth doll in 1906. His *Stockener Doll* had a cloth head painted with oil paints. It didn't have a wig.

Käthe Kruse Imitators

Käthe Kruse's success with her new doll caught the attention of manufacturers. Imitators wanted to have a piece of the pie. They didn't realize how difficult it was to produce the quality of Käthe Kruse dolls.

The manufacturer of Bing Dolls went too far in copying Kruse dolls. They were even referred to as "imitations of the Käthe Kruse dolls." Käthe Kruse decided to go to court.

After two appeals, Käthe Kruse won the Bing court case before the Imperial Court in Leipzig in 1925. It was a fundamental case attributing a toy with artistic origin rights for the first time. Bing Dolls still appear today and in excellent condition, they are worth around $240.

They were copies of Kruse *Doll I,* but copies didn't have the same beauty or quality. One is pictured on page 111.

Prices, Yesterday and Today

Käthe Kruse dolls weren't inexpensive even 50 years ago. Not everyone could afford one because of the hand labor involved. In 1927, a well-clothed *Doll I* cost 29.50 marks. *Träumerchen* in a shoulder-strap dress cost 56.50 marks. *Doll VIII* cost 44.50 marks in 1939. A 21-inch (52cm) doll like *Doll VIII,* cost $172 in the 1981-82 price list. This is 10 times the price of 1939.

An early *Doll I* with sewn-on thumbs and wide hips in good condition and original clothing brings between $480 and $560; a *Doll VIII* about $360; and a *Doll XII* about $400. A very old *Träumerchen* with cloth head costs the most. Collectors pay around $1,400 to $1,600. The same doll with a magnesite head costs around $960. With a more recent plastic head, the doll costs around $240. All prices are based on a doll in good condition.

Dolls cost less if the noses are almost worn out or if they have large cracks on their face or on their heads. Dolls with broken paint layers, severely damaged or badly stuffed bodies are also less expensive.

Doll I with cloth showing through the thinly applied paint is an exception that involves nostalgic charm instead of a lesser value.

Early Käthe Kruse *Doll I*, left, next to a new Bing Doll of the 1920s, right. Imitation doll is not as beautifully painted, and in no degree as well-crafted as the original.

Show-Window Doll Photographs

Käthe Kruse's Show-Window Dolls became very popular. People have admired the beautiful figures that displayed the latest fashions some years ago but didn't know who made them. Show-Window Dolls are discussed on pages 52 to 61.

The public is becoming aware of this great work of Käthe Kruse, which was possible because of the support of her children. It is appropriate to devote a small gallery of photographs to these interesting dolls depicting children and adults. These dolls are growing in popularity as collector items.

Show-Window Doll, *Friedebald*, 40 inches (100cm) tall, from the early 1930s, modeled from the bust by Igor von Jakimow. This is a Figure A according to the description on page 54. This doll almost looks like the living Friedebald.

Two show-window children, *Friedebald* and his brother, in a harmless wrestling match. Their sister looks on as she holds her doll.

The show-window girl *Gundula* designed by Sofie Rehbinder-Kruse. Shown here with *Mäcke.* Both from the 1940s.

A group of Käthe Kruse show-window figures. The picture is from an old Kruse brochure.

A charming group of Show-Window Dolls that received the gold medal at the 1937 Paris World Exhibition. The central figure of this group is the adult *Margarete*. It was designed by Sofie after the actress Liane Haid.

Show-Window Doll *Elisabeth* in a Bavarian dirndl shop.

Marietta, **Show-Window Doll, Figure C, from the 1950s. Ball-joints allowed her to execute almost all human poses.**

Doll-Room Dolls from 1915-16

Käthe Kruse designed the heads of these 4-inch (10cm) dolls based on busts Max Kruse made of his parents, siblings and children. They were manufactured for only a few years.

These scenes were possible because the dolls had movable skeletons. Arranged and photographed by Sofie Rehbinder-Kruse.

Doll I appeared on a post-card series in color and black and white, 5 years after its premiere.

Wer will unter die Soldaten . . .

Kriegsberichterstatter.

Post card written by daughter Maria to Käthe Kruse. It is postmarked Oct. 7, 1916.

Käthe Kruse Dolls on Color Post Cards

Top, *Flower and Dish Market*, a post-card scene with five *Schlenkerchen*. Bottom, siblings of *Doll I* play merchant.

Käthe Kruse Dolls in Paintings

Käthe Kruse dolls inspired artists from the beginning. This 20x24" (50x60cm) oil painting by Ritta Boemm from around 1916 expresses the dolls' characteristics.

Käthe Kruse Dolls in Books

Below is an overview of some of the most important books about Käthe Kruse and her world-famous dolls.

Left: This picture book from the 1920s with illustrations of *Doll I* is rare.

Above and right: The 1951 autobiography of Käthe Kruse is a record of her life and her dolls. A revised edition appeared in 1982.

Above and left: In *Kuddelmuddel,* Käthe Kruse tells charming tales about her own children, her dolls and especially about her Show-Window Dolls. An excerpt is on the opposite page.

How Träumerchen Was Born

The Doll Siblings, by Käthe Kruse
(An excerpt from the book *Kuddelmuddel.*)

Like all babies, *Träumerchen* was born, except it was a doll baby. It happened when I was holding my youngest, my delightful Maxl-Baby, in my arms. You can't imagine how much I loved him. Everyone of you has once been a Maxl-Baby. Because he was the youngest, he was the best and the sweetest in the world. All the youngest are the best.

Because I was so happy with him, old Dr. Wagner looked at me thoughtfully. He was a good, kind doctor. He had seen so much motherly bliss and motherly pain. He was glad this Maxl-Baby was really the most beloved of all. And why not? He probably thought everyone has his turn, just don't push too much.

Dr. Wagner has been dead for a long time. Anyway, there he was looking at me and little Maxl, and he said, "Look, you have to make a doll like that, for instruction in baby care! What we have now is a miserable leather pouch filled with sand, or worse. After all, you are a woman and a blissful mother as well. So, do something for infant care!"

I wanted to serve science this way. As I warmed Maxl's tiny foot with my left hand and stroked his little head with my right hand, I continued to let the doctor talk. I was no longer listening because at that moment *Träumerchen* was born. It developed in my imagination. It became soft, warm, heavy, helpless and sweet and it slept—just as Maxl did in my arms. No one should ever treat it roughly, that was the most important thing. It should be sweet—just like my own, just like Maxl!

I could tell thousands of stories about it. It doesn't matter if I tell a few more, does it? You have to let me brag some! That's a condition! That's why you write storybooks.

Now, let's pretend *Träumerchen* has grown. But first we have to put him in his cradle! He had a beautiful wicker cradle because I just loved wicker baby carriages. Sofie, that's Maxl-Baby's big sister, had done some sewing on it and cleaned it up. It was decorated with brightly flowered batiste and had wide, pink edging.

There were tears shed because of this edging. Someone told Sofie Maxl's basket had to be decorated with blue because he was a boy. Blue is for boys, and girls have everything in pink.

But Maxl-Baby had a dark complexion and little dark hints of curls and dark-black eyes. Light blue wouldn't go at all. Such a dark-complected child must have everything in pink. He practically cried out for pink. That was terribly important to me. Maxl himself, of course, wasn't crying out for pink at all. It made no difference to him whether he was dressed in blue or pink. But Sofie shrugged her shoulders and sewed a pink batiste band around the little basket. My goodness, she didn't find it that important after all. But mothers are, as Sofie said, sometimes "a little nuts."

When Maxl-Baby was 9 or 10 months old, he often sat alone in his carriage. His sister Sofie and all his other brothers and sisters were in school. Maxl-Baby had a bunch of brothers and sisters. He couldn't count them, but he recognized all of them with a friendly smile. But they were gone so often! And Mommy wasn't home either, for Mommy had to go to work again. Because he had to sit alone in his pink basket, he wanted to raise a bit of a protest about the shortcomings of this world. After all, this is the most sacred right of all babies.

Then suddenly the door opened softly and in came the big doll *Ilsebill.*

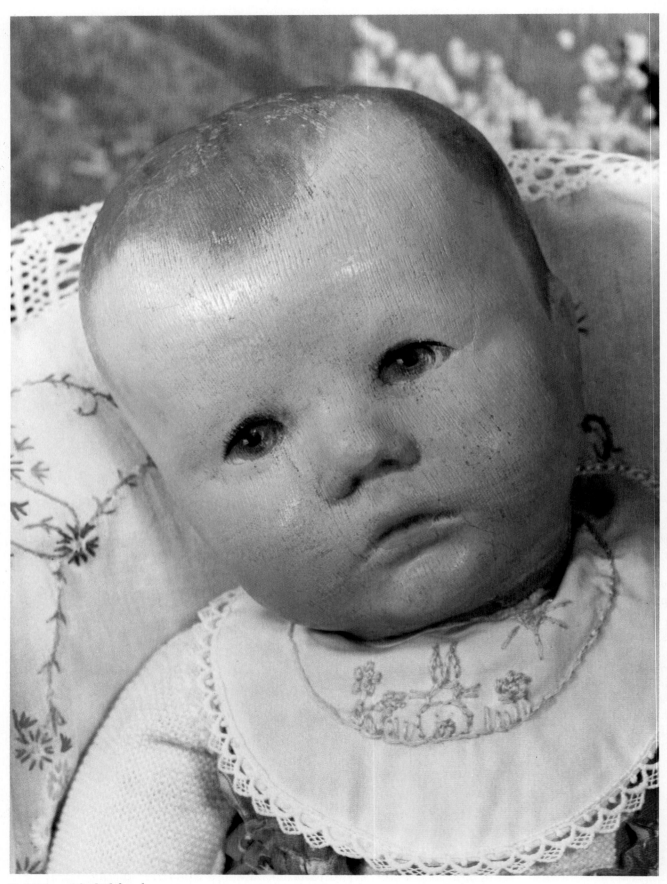

Du Mein with cloth head.

She was so sweet and friendly. She was a show-window child and, therefore, very mobile. I've already explained to you what a show-window child is. *Ilsebill* came over to Maxl-Baby's carriage. She took the little animal that was lying on his blanket with her hand and danced it about before Maxl's eyes, which were still full of tears. *Ilsebill* sang *Eiapopeia*, turned and rocked and little Maxl smiled and crowed. It was wonderful!

At this moment, Michael came home from school. This was not the doll-boy Michael, but Maxl's real live brother Michael. He had just received a camera. It was actually Mommy's camera, but since he had broken it, it had become his. At this moment it was fixed and it worked. Michael, who never in his life let himself be surprised, took a picture. He took the pretty picture before the little doll princess *Ilsebill* got stiff again with fright. Living people aren't permitted to see that dolls can become alive.

Only occasionally can a very good little doll mother experience this. But then no one wants to believe it. But Michael experienced it, and he took a picture. Otherwise, how would that picture get into this book I ask you?

"Oh Mommy," calls Johanna. She is a living sister of Maxl and a very good child. "Oh Mommy, you can sure make things up!"

"What do you mean?" I had to ask. "What did I make up? It's right there, all to be seen in black and white. She must have stood right there!"

Oh, children, give me a kiss, everyone together! I like to kiss so much and to tell stories about dolls.

Index

8.423508929571